JUMP Math 2.2

Book 2 Part 2 of 2

Contents

jump math

MULTIPLYING POTENTIAL.

JUMP Math
Toronto, Canada
www.jumpmath.org

Writers: Dr. John Mighton, Dr. Sindi Sabourin, Dr. Anna Klebanov
Cover Design: Blakeley Words+Pictures
Text Design: Pam Lostracco
Layout: Pam Lostracco, Ilyana Martinez, Rita Camacho
Illustrations: Pam Lostracco
Cover Photograph: © iStockphoto.com/Michael Valdez

ISBN: 978-1-897120-66-8

Seventh printing June 2013

¹Estimates were made using the Environmental Defense Paper Calculator.

This book was manufactured without the use of additional coatings or processes, and was assembled using the latest equipment to achieve almost zero waste. Manufacturing this book in Canada ensures compliance with strict environmental practices and eliminates the need for international freight, which is a major contributor to global air pollution.

Printed and bound in Canada

Welcome to JUMP Math

Entering the world of JUMP Math means believing that every child has the capacity to be fully numerate and to love math. Founder and mathematician John Mighton has used this premise to develop his innovative teaching method. The resulting materials isolate and describe concepts so clearly and incrementally that everyone can understand them.

JUMP Math is comprised of workbooks, teacher's guides, evaluation materials, outreach programs, tutoring support through schools and community organizations, and provincial curriculum correlations. All of this is presented on the JUMP Math website: **www.jumpmath.org**.

Teacher's guides are available on the website for free use. Read the introduction to the teacher's guides before you begin using these materials. This will ensure that you understand both the philosophy and the methodology of JUMP Math. The workbooks are designed for use by children, with adult guidance. Each child will have unique needs and it is important to provide the child with the appropriate support and encouragement as he or she works through the material.

Allow children to discover the concepts on the worksheets by themselves as much as possible. Mathematical discoveries can be made in small, incremental steps. The discovery of a new step is like untangling the parts of a puzzle. It is exciting and rewarding.

Children will need to answer the questions marked with a ▤ in a notebook. Grid paper and notebooks should always be on hand for answering extra questions or when additional room for calculation is needed. Grid paper is also available in the BLM section of the Teacher's Guide.

Contents

PART 2
Number Sense

Patterns and Algebra

Measurement

Geometry

Probability and Data Management

Skip Counting

Count by 2s and colour the numbers that you say.

☐ Start at **2** and colour the numbers **blue**.

☐ Start at **1** and colour the numbers **red**.

1	2	3	4	5	6	7	8	9	10
11	12	13	14	15	16	17	18	19	20
21	22	23	24	25	26	27	28	29	30
31	32	33	34	35	36	37	38	39	40

The blue numbers have ones digit ____, ____, ____, ____, or ____.

The red numbers have ones digit ____, ____, ____, ____, or ____.

☐ Count by 2s.

2, _____, _____, _____, _____, _____, *14*

42, _____, _____, _____, _____, _____, _____

86, _____, _____, _____, *94*, _____, _____

1, _____, _____, _____, *9*, _____, _____

61, _____, _____, _____, _____, _____, _____

☐ Count back by 2s.

86, *84*, _____, _____, _____, *76*, _____

☐ Start at 5 and count by 5s. Colour the numbers that you say.

1	2	3	4	5	6	7	8	9	10
11	12	13	14	15	16	17	18	19	20
21	22	23	24	25	26	27	28	29	30

The coloured numbers have ones digit ___ or ___.

☐ Count by 5s.

0 __5__ _____ _____ _____ _____ _____

60 __65__ _____ _____ _____ _____ _____

70 _____ _____ _____ _____ __95__ _____

☐ Count back by 5s.

30 __25__ _____ _____ _____ _____ _____

80 _____ _____ _____ _____ __55__ _____

100 _____ _____ __85__ _____ _____ _____

☐ Count by 2s and then by 1s to see how many.

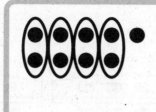

2 4 6 7

_7_

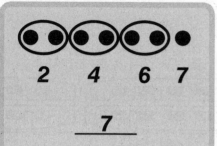

____

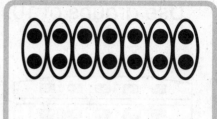

____

____

☐ Count by 5s and then by 1s to see how many.

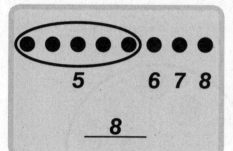

5   6 7 8

_8_

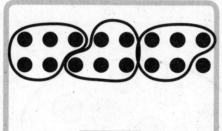

____

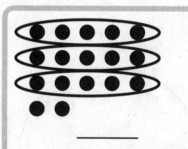

____

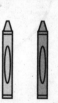

____

There are _____ letters in the alphabet.

☐ Count how many.
   Use groups of 10.

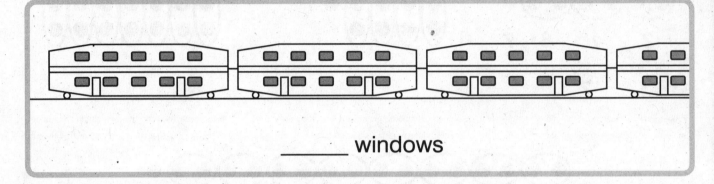

_____ windows

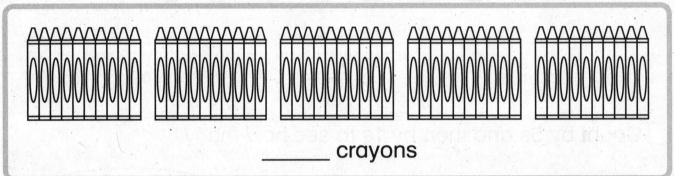

_____ crayons

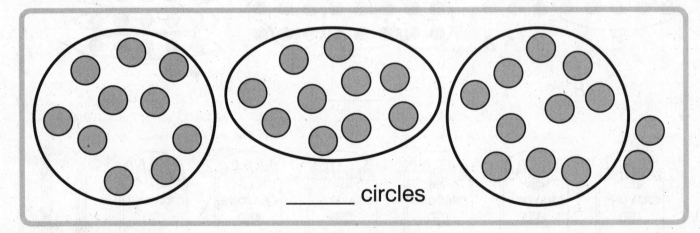

_____ circles

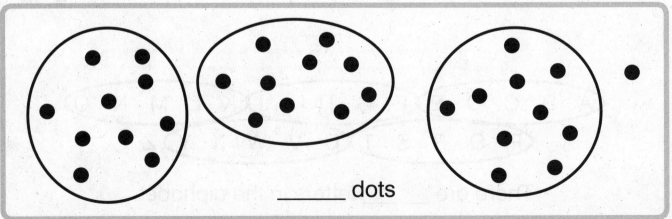

_____ dots

Count by 10s and colour the numbers that you say.

☐ Start at **10** and colour the numbers **red**.
☐ Start at **7** and colour the numbers **blue**.

1	2	3	4	5	6	7	8	9	10
11	12	13	14	15	16	17	18	19	20
21	22	23	24	25	26	27	28	29	30
31	32	33	34	35	36	37	38	39	40

The red numbers have ones digit _____.

The blue numbers have ones digit _____.

☐ Count by 10s.

20 _____ _____ **50** _____ _____ _____

40 _____ _____ _____ **90** _____

37 _____ _____ **77** _____ _____

22 _____ _____ _____ _____ _____

15 _____ _____ _____ _____ _____

If you can count back from 10 by 1s:

10   9   8   7   ...

Then you can count back from 100 by 10s:

100   90   80   70   ...

and from 93 by 10s:

93   83   73   63   ...

☐ Count back by 10s.

100 _____ _____ _____ _____ _____

53 _____ _____ _____ _____ _____

80 _____ _____ _____ _____ _____

76 _____ _____ _____ _____ _____

☐ Count back by 10s.
   Use a metre stick or a tape measure.

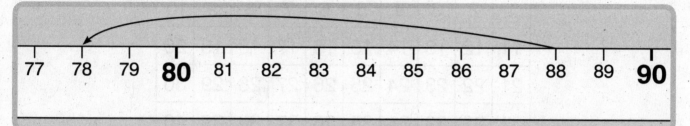

77 78 79 **80** 81 82 83 84 85 86 87 88 89 **90**

88   _78_   _____ _____ _____ _____ _____

92   _____ _____ _____ _____ _____ _____

83   _____ _____ _____ _____ _____ _____

96   _____ _____ _____ _____ _____ _____

75   _____ _____ _____ _____ _____ _____

85   _____ _____ _____ _____ _____ _____

87   _____ _____ _____ _____ _____ _____

64   _____ _____ _____ _____ _____ _____

☐ Use a hundreds chart to count back by 10s.

1	2	3	4	5	6	7	8	9	10
11	12	13	14	15	16	17	18	19	20
21	22	23	24	25	26	27	28	29	30
31	32	33	34	35	36	37	38	39	40
41	42	43	44	45	46	47	48	49	50
51	52	53	54	55	56	57	58	59	60
61	62	63	64	65	66	67	68	69	70
71	72	73	74	75	76	77	78	79	80
81	82	83	84	85	86	87	88	89	90
91	92	93	94	95	96	97	98	99	100

97 ____ ____ ____ ____ ____ ____

76 ____ ____ ____ ____ ____ ____

82 ____ ____ ____ ____ ____ ____

99 ____ ____ ____ ____ ____ ____

Is counting back by 10s easier using a hundreds chart or a number line? Explain. _____

_____

Closer To

☐ Write 0 or 10.

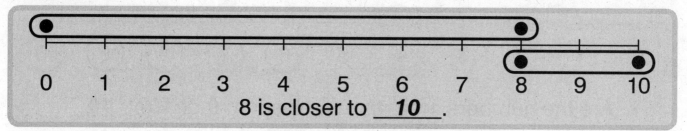

8 is closer to __10__.

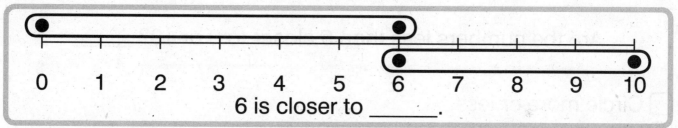

4 is closer to _____.

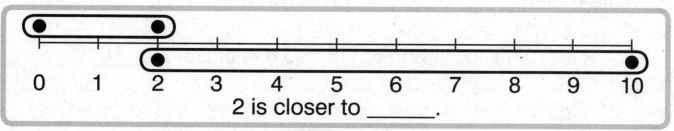

6 is closer to _____.

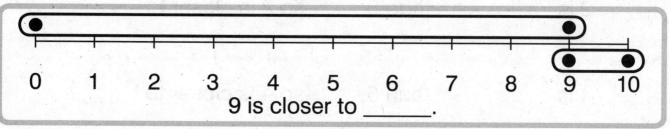

2 is closer to _____.

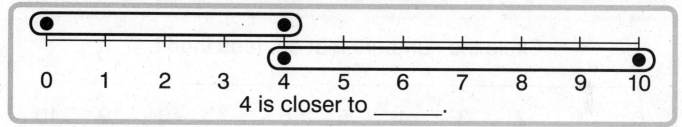

9 is closer to _____.

☐ **Bonus:** Show the number that is **equally** close to 0 and 10.

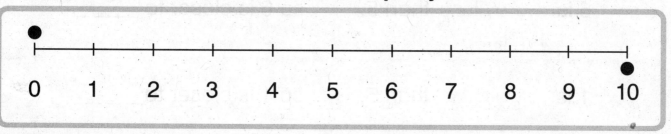

Circle the numbers that are **more** than 5.

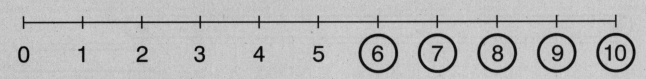

Are the numbers more than 5 closer to 0 or 10? __10__

Circle the numbers that are **less** than 5.

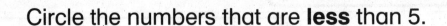

Are the numbers less than 5 closer to 0 or 10? _____

☐ Circle more or less.
☐ Write 0 or 10.

8 is ⟨more⟩/ less than 5,   so 8 is closer to __10__.

2 is more / less than 5,   so 2 is closer to _____.

4 is more / less than 5,   so 4 is closer to _____.

6 is more / less than 5,   so 6 is closer to _____.

1 is more / less than 5,   so 1 is closer to _____.

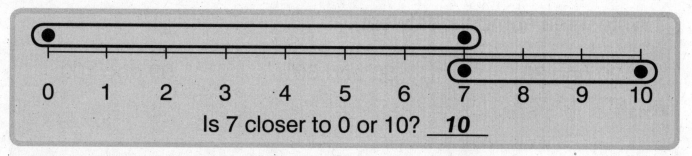

Is 7 closer to 0 or 10? **10**

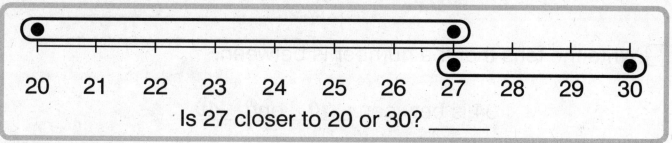

Is 27 closer to 20 or 30? _____

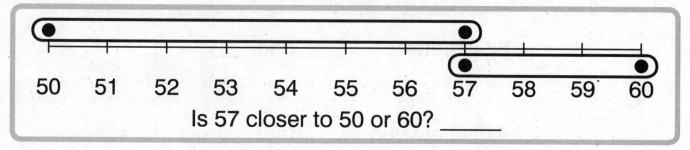

Is 57 closer to 50 or 60? _____

☐ Circle the correct number.

Is 87 closer to 80 or (90)?	Is 97 closer to 90 or 100?

Is 3 closer to 0 or 10?	Is 9 closer to 0 or 10?
Is 13 closer to 10 or 20?	Is 29 closer to 20 or 30?
Is 43 closer to 40 or 50?	Is 99 closer to 90 or 100?
Is 73 closer to 70 or 80?	Is 69 closer to 60 or 70?

Is 46 closer to 40 or 50?	Is 24 closer to 20 or 30?

Is 52 closer to 50 or 60?	Is 38 closer to 30 or 40?

☐ Write three numbers between…

| 20 and 30 | 50 and 60 | 90 and 100 |

☐ Write the tens that the number is between.

34 is between __30__ and __40__ .

86 is between _____ and _____ .

41 is between _____ and _____ .

☐ Find the ten that the number is closest to by using 5.

37 is between __30__ and __40__ .
7 is (more)/ less than 5.
37 is closest to __40__ .

62 is between ____ and ____ .
2 is more / less than 5.
62 is closest to ____ .

26 is between ____ and ____ .
6 is more / less than 5.
26 is closest to ____ .

84 is between ____ and ____ .
4 is more / less than 5.
84 is closest to ____ .

53 is closest to _____ .

79 is closest to _____ .

Estimating Numbers

10 dots are circled.

☐ Estimate the closest ten.
☐ Group by 10s to check.

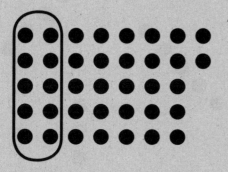

Estimate: ___30___

Check: ___37___

Closest ten: ___40___

Estimate: _____

Check: _____

Closest ten: _____

Estimate: _____

Check: _____

Closest ten: _____

Estimate: _____

Check: _____

Closest ten: _____

10 dots are circled.

☐ Estimate the closest ten. _____
☐ Circle 2 more groups of 10. Estimate again. _____

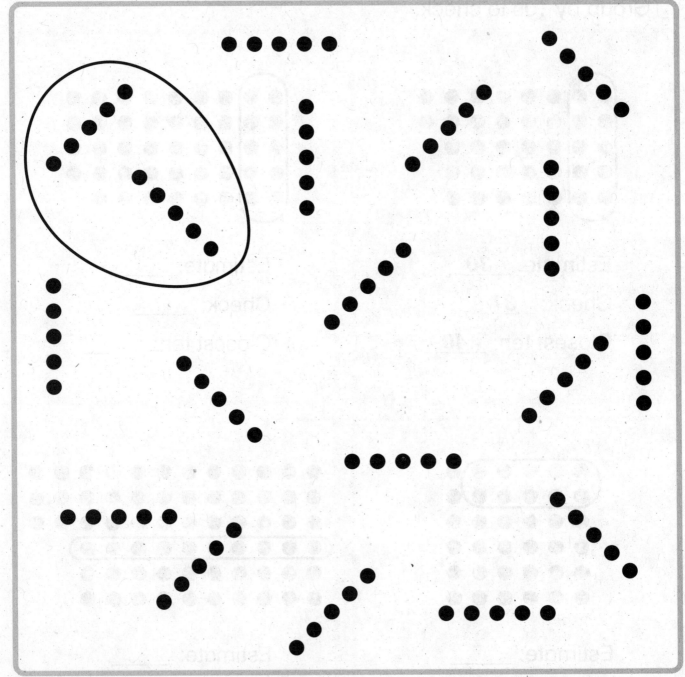

☐ Group by 10s to count. _____
Did circling more groups of 10 improve your estimate? yes / no
☐ Why do you think that happened?

Even and Odd

The number of stars is **even** if you can pair them up.
The number of stars is **odd** if you cannot.

- ☐ Count the stars.
- ☐ Pair them up.
- ☐ Write even or odd.

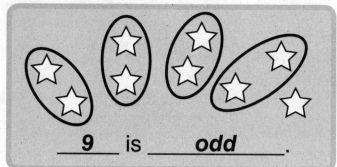

____9____ is ____*odd*____.

_____ is _____.

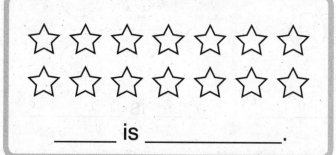

_____ is _____.

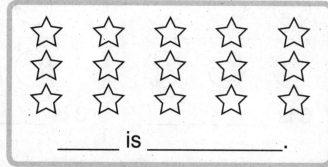

_____ is _____.

_____ is _____.

_____ is _____.

Can you divide the people into 2 **equal** teams?

Yes ⟶ The number of people is **even**.

No ⟶ The number of people is **odd**.

☐ Fill in the blanks.

8 is ____**even**____.

I don't have a team!

7 is ____**odd**____.

6 is _____.

3 is _____.

___ is _____.

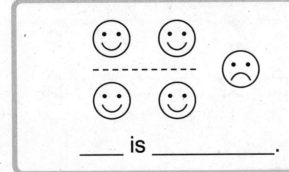

___ is _____.

___ is _____.

___ is _____.

___ is _____.

16

Number Sense 2-48

Patterns with Even and Odd

☐ Pair objects up.
☐ Write **even** or **odd**.

1 is _____.

2 is _____.

3 is _____.

4 is _____.

5 is _____.

6 is _____.

7 is _____.

8 is _____.

9 is _____.

☐ Write **O** for odd and **E** for even.
☐ Extend both patterns.

1	2	3	4	5	6	7	8	9	10
O	*E*	___	___	___	___	___	___	___	___

11	12	13	14	15	16			
						___	___	___

___   ___   ___   ___   ___

Even and odd numbers alternate.

☐ Shade the even numbers.
☐ Circle the odd numbers.

1	2	3	4	5	6	7	8	9	10
11	12	13	14	15	16	17	18	19	20

☐ Write the **ones digits** of the **shaded** numbers.
☐ Extend the pattern.

___ ___ ___ ___ ___

___ ___ ___ ___ ___

___ ___ ___ ___ ___

☐ Write the **ones digits** of the **circled** numbers.
☐ Extend the pattern.

___ ___ ___ ___ ___

___ ___ ___ ___ ___

___ ___ ___ ___ ___

Even numbers have ones digit _____, _____, _____, _____, or _____.

Odd numbers have ones digit _____, _____, _____, _____, or _____.

Even numbers have ones digit 0, 2, 4, 6, or 8.
Odd numbers have ones digit 1, 3, 5, 7, or 9.

☐ Circle the even numbers.
☐ Underline the odd numbers.

| 1 | ② | 3 | 4 | 5 | 6 | 7 | 8 | 9 | 10 |

| 2 | 4 | 6 | 8 | 10 | 12 | 14 | 16 | 18 | 20 |

| 5 | 10 | 15 | 20 | 25 | 30 | 35 | 40 | 45 | 50 |

| 10 | 20 | 30 | 40 | 50 | 60 | 70 | 80 | 90 | 100 |

17   4   26   47
      94   61
   17
         43
9   3   71
         34
   94   90
81   18   26   62

☐ **Bonus:** Describe all the patterns you see.

☐ Write the next even number.

| 56 _____ | 60 _____ | 74 _____ | 12 _____ |

| 36 _____ | 46 _____ | 52 _____ | 70 _____ |

☐ Write the next odd number.

| 57 _____ | 61 _____ | 75 _____ | 33 _____ |

| 25 _____ | 47 _____ | 23 _____ | 91 _____ |

☐ Write the even number before.

| _____ 26 | _____ 14 | _____ 38 | _____ 42 |

| _____ 78 | _____ 84 | _____ 12 | _____ 56 |

☐ Write the odd number before.

| _____ 79 | _____ 53 | _____ 65 | _____ 83 |

| _____ 55 | _____ 85 | _____ 99 | _____ 47 |

Patterns in Adding

☐ Separate.
☐ Write the number in different ways.

$6 = 1 + \underline{\textbf{5}}$

$6 = 2 + \underline{\textbf{4}}$

$6 = 3 + \underline{\textbf{3}}$

$10 = 1 + \underline{}$

$10 = 2 + \underline{}$

$10 = 3 + \underline{}$

$10 = 4 + \underline{}$

$10 = 5 + \underline{}$

$7 = 1 + \underline{}$

$7 = 2 + \underline{}$

$7 = 3 + \underline{}$

$8 = 1 + \underline{}$

$8 = 2 + \underline{}$

$8 = 3 + \underline{}$

$8 = 4 + \underline{}$

☐ Write 9 in different ways.

$9 = \underline{} + \underline{}$

$9 = \underline{} + \underline{}$

$9 = \underline{} + \underline{}$

$9 = \underline{} + \underline{}$

Adding Tens and Ones

☐ Write the number as a sum of 10s and 1s.

32 = **10 + 10 + 10 + 1 + 1**	13 =
41 =	22 =

☐ We can write 24 = 20 + 4. Write each number in the same way.

35 = _**30 + 5**_	47 = _____	63 = _____
81 = _____	56 = _____	92 = _____

☐ Add.

40 + 5 = _**45**_	6 + 20 = _____	70 + 1 = _____
8 + 60 = _____	70 + 7 = _____	4 + 50 = _____
30 + 8 = _____	9 + 10 = _____	6 + 80 = _____
7 + 90 = _____	9 + 70 = _____	70 + 9 = _____

☐ Add.

$5 + 2$ = $1 + 1 + 1 + 1 + 1$ + $1 + 1$ = _____

$50 + 20$ = $10 + 10 + 10 + 10 + 10$ + $10 + 10$ = _____

$4 + 4$ = $1 + 1 + 1 + 1$ + $1 + 1 + 1 + 1$ = _____

$40 + 40$ = $10 + 10 + 10 + 10 + 10 + 10 + 10 + 10$ = _____

$2 + 3$ = $1 + 1$ + $1 + 1 + 1$ = _____

$20 + 30$ = $10 + 10$ + $10 + 10 + 10$ = _____

$2 + 6 =$ _____

$20 + 60 =$ _____

$4 + 1 =$ _____

$40 + 10 =$ _____

$5 + 4 =$ _____

$50 + 40 =$ _____

$1 + 5 =$ _____

$10 + 50 =$ _____

$3 + 3 =$ _____

$30 + 30 =$ _____

$3 + 4 =$ _____

$30 + 40 =$ _____

$1 + 3 + 2 =$ _____

$10 + 30 + 20 =$ _____

$2 + 3 + 2 + 1 =$ _____

$20 + 30 + 20 + 10 =$ _____

Adding in Two Ways

☐ Separate the dots in two different places.
☐ Write an addition sentence.

$\underline{\quad 3 \quad} + \underline{\quad 6 \quad} = \underline{\quad 5 \quad} + \underline{\quad 4 \quad}$

___ + ___ = ___ + ___

___ + ___ = ___ + ___

___ + ___ = ___ + ___

_____

_____

Count the shaded boxes in each row or column.
How many shaded boxes altogether?

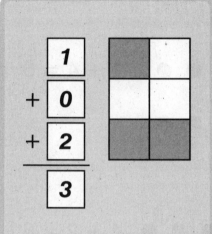

$$1 + 0 + 2 = 3$$

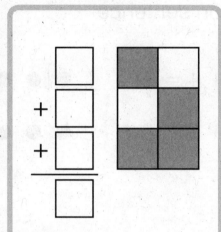

$$\square + \square = \square$$

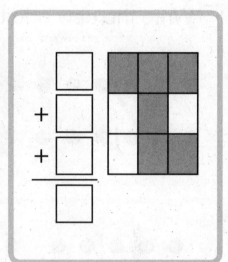

$$\square + \square = \square$$

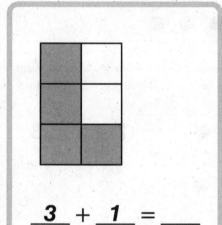

$$\underline{\ 3\ } + \underline{\ 1\ } = \underline{\ \ }$$

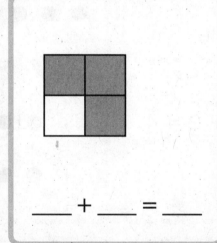

$$\underline{\ \ } + \underline{\ \ } = \underline{\ \ }$$

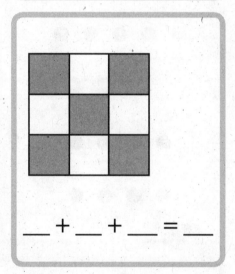

$$\underline{\ } + \underline{\ } + \underline{\ } = \underline{\ }$$

Write 2 addition sentences for the total number of shaded boxes.

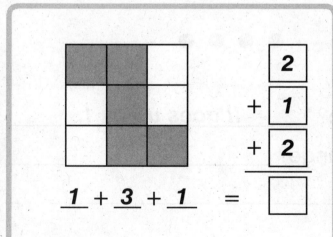

$$\underline{\ 1\ } + \underline{\ 3\ } + \underline{\ 1\ } = \square$$

$$2 + 1 + 2 = \square$$

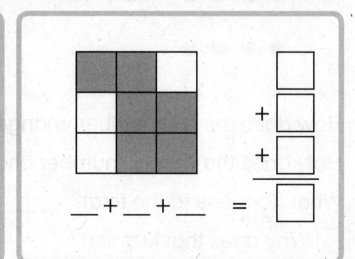

$$\underline{\ } + \underline{\ } + \underline{\ } = \square$$

$$\square + \square + \square = \square$$

Addition Strategies

☐ Move the line one place to the right ⟶.
☐ Write the new addition sentence.

● ● | ● ● ● ●　2 + 4 = 6

● ● ● | ● ● ●　**3 + 3 = 6**

● | ● ● ● ●　1 + 4 = 5

● ● ● ● ●

● ● ● | ● ●　3 + 2 = 5

● ● ● ● ●

● ● ● ● | ● ●　4 + 2 = 6

● ● ● ● ● ●

● ● | ● ●　2 + 2 = 4

● ● ● ●

● | ● ●　1 + 2 = 3

● ● ●

| ● ● ● ●　0 + 4 = 4

● ● ● ●

● ● ● | ●　3 + 1 = 4

● ● ● ●

How does the first number change? _____ *It goes up by 1.*

How does the second number change? _____

What happens to the total? _____

☐ Why does that happen?

Add and subtract 1 to make a new number sentence.

$2 + 5 = 7$

+1	−1	
3	+ 4	= 7

$3 + 8 = 11$

+1	−1	
☐	+ ☐	= ☐

$6 + 3 = 9$

+1	−1	
☐	+ ☐	= ☐

$8 + 3 = 11$

+1	−1	
☐	+ ☐	= ☐

$5 + 9 = 14$

☐	☐	
☐	+ ☐	= ☐

$5 + 2 = 7$

☐	☐	
☐	+ ☐	= ☐

$7 + 11 = 18$

☐	☐	
☐	+ ☐	= ☐

$11 + 7 = 18$

☐	☐	
☐	+ ☐	= ☐

Finish the addition sentence.

$6 + 11 = 7 + \underline{\hspace{2em}}$

$8 + 4 = 9 + \underline{\hspace{2em}}$

☐ Draw a model.
☐ Move the line one place to the left ⟵.
☐ Write the new addition sentence.

● ● | ● ● ● ● 2 + 4 = 6 ● | ● ● ● ● ● *1 + 5 = 6*	● ● | ● ● ● 2 + 3 = 5
4 + 1 = 5	4 + 2 = 6
2 + 2 = 4	1 + 2 = 3
2 + 1 = 3	4 + 0 = 4

How does the first number change? _____

How does the second number change? _____

What happens to the total? _____

☐ Why does that happen?

first number   second number

● | ● ● ● ● ●   1 + 5 = 6

● ● ● ● | ● ●   4 + 2 = 6

The first number went _____**up**_____ by __**3**__.

The second number went _____**down**_____ by __**3**__.

● ● | ● ● ● ● ●   2 + 5 = 7

● ● ● ● | ● ● ●   4 + 3 = 7

The first number went _____ by ____.

The second number went _____ by ____.

● ● ● ● ● | ● ●   5 + 2 = 7

● | ● ● ● ● ● ●   1 + 6 = 7

The first number went _____ by ____.

The second number went _____ by ____.

☐ Change both numbers in opposite ways.
☐ Write the addition sentences.
☐ Did the total change?

3   4   3 + 4 = __7__

+ 2   − 2

5   2   __5__ + __2__ = __7__

Did the total change? __No__

6   4   6 + 4 = ____

− 3   + ☐

☐   ☐   ____ + ____ = ____

Did the total change? ____

0   9   0 + 9 = ____

+ 4   − ☐

☐   ☐   ____ + ____ = ____

Did the total change? ____

6   2   6 + 2 = ____

− 2   + ☐

☐   ☐   ____ + ____ = ____

Did the total change? ____

Using 10 to Add

☐ Use the group of 10 to help you add.

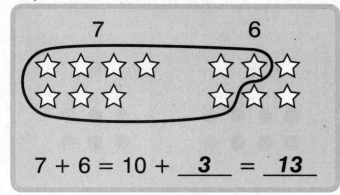

7 + 6 = 10 + __3__ = __13__

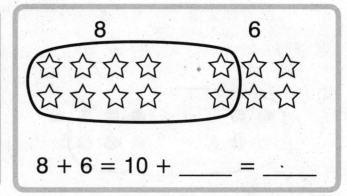

8 + 6 = 10 + _____ = _____

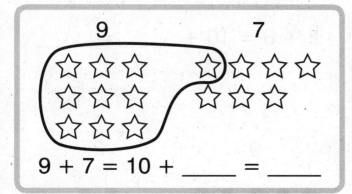

9 + 7 = 10 + _____ = _____

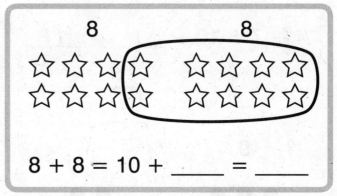

8 + 8 = 10 + _____ = _____

7 + 5 = 10 + _____ = _____

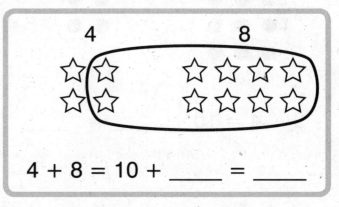

4 + 8 = 10 + _____ = _____

☐ Sara groups 10 in two ways. Does she get the same answer?

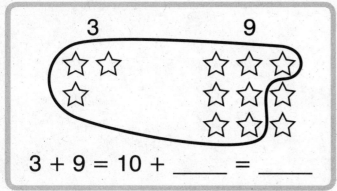

3 + 9 = 10 + _____ = _____

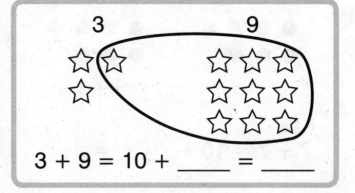

3 + 9 = 10 + _____ = _____

☐ Circle a group of 10.
☐ Use 10 to add.

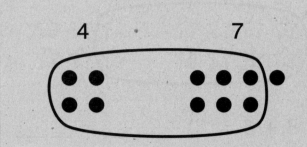

4   7

$4 + 7 = 10 + \underline{\ \textit{1}\ } = \underline{\ \textit{11}\ }$

8   6

$8 + 6 = 10 + \underline{\quad} = \underline{\quad}$

9   4

$9 + 4 = 10 + \underline{\quad} = \underline{\quad}$

9   2

$9 + 2 = 10 + \underline{\quad} = \underline{\quad}$

7   7

$7 + 7 = 10 + \underline{\quad} = \underline{\quad}$

Make your own.

⬜ **Use 10 to add.**

$$8 + 6 = 10 + \underline{\;4\;} = \underline{\;14\;}$$

$$7 + 5 = 10 + \underline{\quad} = \underline{\quad}$$

$$7 + 9 = 10 + \underline{\quad} = \underline{\quad}$$

⬜ **Now finish the model, then add.**

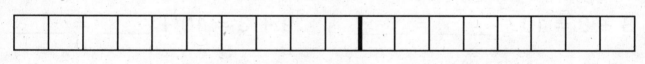

$$6 + 5 = 10 + \underline{\quad} = \underline{\quad}$$

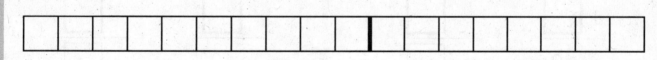

$$9 + 5 = 10 + \underline{\quad} = \underline{\quad}$$

Does using 10 make adding easier? _____

Explain. _____

_____

📓 **Which two answers are the same? Why did that happen?**

☐ What makes 10 with the first number?
  Subtract that amount from the second number.
☐ Use 10 to add.

first number   second number
        ↓   ↓
       8   5

+ [2]   – [2]

10   [3]

8 + 5 = 10 + __3__ = __13__

---

       8   7

+ [ ]   – [ ]

10   [ ]

8 + 7 = 10 + ____ = ____

---

       8   8

+ [ ]   – [ ]

10   [ ]

8 + 8 = 10 + ____ = ____

---

       9   3

+ [ ]   – [ ]

10   [ ]

9 + 3 = 10 + ____ = ____

---

       3   9

+ [ ]   – [ ]

10   [ ]

3 + 9 = 10 + ____ = ____

---

       8   6

+ [ ]   – [ ]

10   [ ]

8 + 6 = 10 + ____ = ____

📓 Which two questions have the same answer?
  Why did that happen?
  Which question was easier?

☐ What makes 10 with the first number?
   Subtract that amount from the second number.
☐ Use 10 to add.

first number   second number
      ↓   ↓
      8   7

   + [2]   − [2]
   ─────   ─────
     10   [5]

      so 8 + 7 = __15__

      6   9

   + [ ]   − [ ]
   ─────   ─────
     10   [ ]

      so 6 + 9 = _____

      7   6

   + [ ]   − [ ]
   ─────   ─────
     10   [ ]

      so 7 + 6 = _____

      9   8

   + [ ]   − [ ]
   ─────   ─────
     10   [ ]

      so 9 + 8 = _____

How do you know that 8 + 6 has the same answer as 10 + 4?

_____

_____

| 9 + 5 = ___ | 8 + 8 = ___ | 7 + 5 = ___ | 7 + 7 = ___ |

☐ Add 1 to one of the numbers.
☐ Subtract 1 from the other number.
☐ Solve the new addition sentence.

$$32 + 9$$
$$= \underline{31} + \underline{10} = \underline{41}$$

$$19 + 8$$
$$= \underline{} + \underline{} = \underline{}$$

$$7 + 29$$
$$= \underline{} + \underline{} = \underline{}$$

$$27 + 19$$
$$= \underline{} + \underline{} = \underline{}$$

$$19 + 16$$
$$= \underline{} + \underline{} = \underline{}$$

$$29 + 6$$
$$= \underline{} + \underline{} = \underline{}$$

$$18 + 9$$
$$= \underline{} + \underline{} = \underline{}$$

$$9 + 36$$
$$= \underline{} + \underline{} = \underline{}$$

$$9 + 47$$
$$= \underline{} + \underline{} = \underline{}$$

$$38 + 19$$
$$= \underline{} + \underline{} = \underline{}$$

☐ Sam has to solve $27 + 29$. He says $26 + 30$ has the same answer. Explain why he is right.

☐ Which problem is easier, $27 + 29$ or $26 + 30$? Explain.

Number Sense 2-54

Make a new addition problem by adding and subtracting 2.
Solve the new addition problem.

$18 + 15$
$= \underline{\textbf{20}} + \underline{\hspace{1.5em}} = \underline{\hspace{1.5em}}$

$14 + 28$
$= \underline{\hspace{1.5em}} + \underline{\textbf{30}} = \underline{\hspace{1.5em}}$

$37 + 48$
$= \underline{\hspace{1.5em}} + \underline{\textbf{50}} = \underline{\hspace{1.5em}}$

$68 + 24$
$= \underline{\textbf{70}} + \underline{\hspace{1.5em}} = \underline{\hspace{1.5em}}$

$42 + 54$
$= \underline{\textbf{40}} + \underline{\hspace{1.5em}} = \underline{\hspace{1.5em}}$

$72 + 17$
$= \underline{\textbf{70}} + \underline{\hspace{1.5em}} = \underline{\hspace{1.5em}}$

$56 + 32$
$= \underline{\hspace{1.5em}} + \underline{\hspace{1.5em}} = \underline{\hspace{1.5em}}$

$28 + 45$
$= \underline{\hspace{1.5em}} + \underline{\hspace{1.5em}} = \underline{\hspace{1.5em}}$

$22 + 35$
$= \underline{\hspace{1.5em}} + \underline{\hspace{1.5em}} = \underline{\hspace{1.5em}}$

$43 + 48$
$= \underline{\hspace{1.5em}} + \underline{\hspace{1.5em}} = \underline{\hspace{1.5em}}$

Using Tens and Ones to Add

How many tens and ones altogether?

☐ Add.

___2___ tens + ___5___ ones

13   +   12   =   ___25___

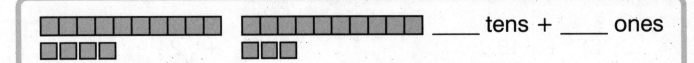

_____ tens + _____ ones

14   +   13   =   _____

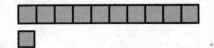

_____ tens + _____ ones

11   +   15   =   _____

☐ Now draw the blocks and add.

_____ tens + _____ ones

12   +   12   =   _____

☐ Make your own problem.

_____ tens + _____ ones

=   _____

□ Add by separating the tens and ones.

23   =   20 + 3
+ 34   =   30 + 4
─────────   ─────────
[57] ←─────   50 + 7

34   =   30 + 4
+ 15   =   10 + 5
─────────   ─────────
[ ] ←─────   40 + 9

27   =   20 + [ ]
+ 22   =   20 + [ ]
─────────   ─────────
[ ] ←─────   40 + [ ]

35   =   [ ] + [ ]
+ 42   =   [ ] + [ ]
─────────   ─────────
[ ] ←─────   [ ] + [ ]

15   =   [ ] + [ ]
+ 23   =   [ ] + [ ]
─────────   ─────────
[ ] ←─────   [ ] + [ ]

26   =   [ ] + [ ]
+ 13   =   [ ] + [ ]
─────────   ─────────
[ ] ←─────   [ ] + [ ]

34   =   [ ] + [ ]
+ 54   =   [ ] + [ ]
─────────   ─────────
[ ] ←─────   [ ] + [ ]

26   =   [ ] + [ ]
+ 33   =   [ ] + [ ]
─────────   ─────────
[ ] ←─────   [ ] + [ ]

22   =   [ ] + [ ]
14   =   [ ] + [ ]
+ 21   =   [ ] + [ ]
─────────   ─────────
[ ] ←─────   [ ] + [ ]

11   =   [ ] + [ ]
22   =   [ ] + [ ]
+ 33   =   [ ] + [ ]
─────────   ─────────
[ ] ←─────   [ ] + [ ]

⬜ Add by using a tens and ones chart.

	35	tens	ones
	+ 32	3	5
		3	2
	67 ←	6	7

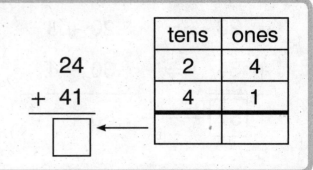

24
+ 41
☐ ←

tens	ones
2	4
4	1

46
+ 31
☐ ←

tens	ones

43
+ 23
☐ ←

tens	ones

27
+ 21
+ 51
☐ ←

tens	ones

31
+ 42
+ 14
☐ ←

tens	ones

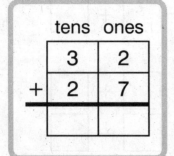

tens	ones
3	2
+ 2	7

tens	ones
4	8
+ 3	1

tens	ones
5	5
+ 2	3

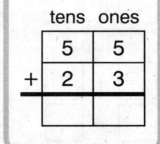

tens	ones
2	2
+ 1	3

📓
37
+ 22

63
+ 16

25
+ 34

31
+ 62

54
+ 34

23
+ 43

Regrouping

☐ Group 10 ones blocks together.
☐ Add.

7   5

$$7 + 5 = 10 + \underline{\ \ 2\ \ } = \underline{\ \ 12\ \ }$$

6   8

$$6 + 8 = 10 + \underline{\qquad} = \underline{\qquad}$$

5   8

$$5 + 8 = 10 + \underline{\qquad} = \underline{\qquad}$$

8   4

$$8 + 4 = 10 + \underline{\qquad} = \underline{\qquad}$$

7   7

$$7 + 7 = 10 + \underline{\qquad} = \underline{\qquad}$$

☐ Group 10 ones blocks together.
How many tens and ones?

☐ Add.

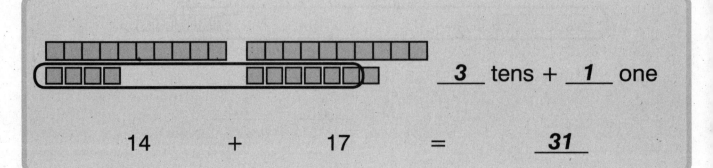

___3___ tens + ___1___ one

14   +   17   =   ___31___

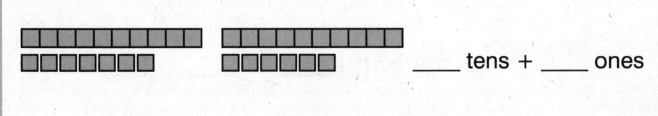

____ tens + ____ ones

17   +   16   =   ____

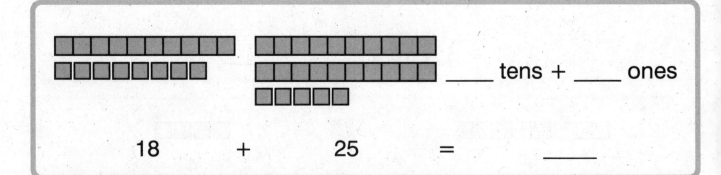

____ tens + ____ ones

18   +   25   =   ____

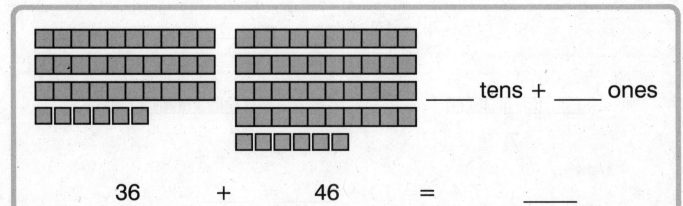

____ tens + ____ ones

36   +   46   =   ____

☐ Trade groups of 10 ones for tens.
☐ Regroup in the next row.

tens	ones
4	27
6	**7**

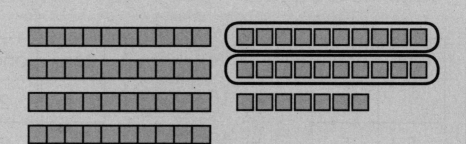

tens	ones
3	12

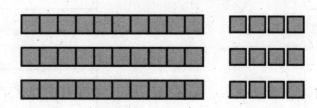

tens	ones
5	21

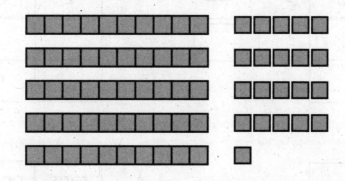

tens	ones
3	15

tens	ones
6	19

tens	ones
4	28

☐ Add the tens and ones.
☐ Regroup in the next row.
☐ Write the answer.

tens	ones
1	6
5	5
6	**11**
7	**1**

16
+ 55
‾‾‾‾
71

tens	ones
1	2
2	9

12
+ 29
‾‾‾‾

tens	ones
2	5
3	8

25
+ 38
‾‾‾‾

tens	ones
5	7
2	6

57
+ 26
‾‾‾‾

tens	ones
2	8
2	6

28
+ 26
‾‾‾‾

tens	ones
2	3
5	2
1	6

23
52
+ 16
‾‾‾‾

The Standard Algorithm for Addition

☐ Add the ones.
☐ Write the tens in the tens column.
☐ Write the ones in the ones column.

---

5 + 9 = ☐**1** ☐**4**

tens ones
☐**1**
  1   5
+ 2 9
☐**4**

---

3 + 8 = ☐**1** ☐**1**

tens ones
☐
  2   3
+ 3 8

---

6 + 4 = ☐**1** ☐**0**

tens ones
☐
  5   6
+ 3 4

---

7 + 5 = ☐ ☐

tens ones
☐
  3   7
+ 2 5

---

6 + 9 = ☐ ☐

tens ones
☐
  1   6
+ 4 9

__ + __ = ☐ ☐

tens ones
☐
  2   7
+ 3 8

☐
  1   4
+ 3 8

☐
  4   7
+ 2 3

☐
  1   5
+ 3 5

☐ Add the ones first.
☐ Then add the tens to find the total.

1 1 5 + 2 9 **4** **4**	☐ 2 3 + 3 8 ☐ ☐	☐ 5 6 + 3 4 ☐ ☐	☐ 2 9 + 1 1 ☐ ☐
☐ 3 7 + 2 5 ☐ ☐	☐ 1 6 + 4 9 ☐ ☐	☐ 2 7 + 3 8 ☐ ☐	☐ 1 5 + 1 9 ☐ ☐
☐ 1 4 + 3 8 ☐ ☐	☐ 4 7 + 2 3 ☐ ☐	☐ 1 5 + 3 5 ☐ ☐	☐ 2 8 + 3 8 ☐ ☐

Regroup only when you need to.
Add using the standard algorithm.

$\boxed{1}$		$\boxed{}$		$\boxed{}$		$\boxed{}$

$$\begin{array}{r} \boxed{1} \\ 1\;\;9 \\ +\;2\;\;6 \\ \hline \boxed{4}\;\boxed{5} \end{array} \qquad \begin{array}{r} \boxed{} \\ 2\;\;5 \\ +\;3\;\;3 \\ \hline \boxed{5}\;\boxed{8} \end{array} \qquad \begin{array}{r} \boxed{} \\ 3\;\;7 \\ +\;2\;\;5 \\ \hline \boxed{}\;\boxed{} \end{array} \qquad \begin{array}{r} \boxed{} \\ 2\;\;3 \\ +\;4\;\;6 \\ \hline \boxed{}\;\boxed{} \end{array}$$

$$\begin{array}{r} \boxed{} \\ 2\;\;9 \\ +\;\;\;\;4 \\ \hline \boxed{}\;\boxed{} \end{array} \qquad \begin{array}{r} \boxed{} \\ 1\;\;3 \\ +\;2\;\;2 \\ \hline \boxed{}\;\boxed{} \end{array} \qquad \begin{array}{r} \boxed{} \\ 4\;\;7 \\ +\;\;\;\;3 \\ \hline \boxed{}\;\boxed{} \end{array} \qquad \begin{array}{r} \boxed{} \\ 8\;\;6 \\ +\;\;\;\;1 \\ \hline \boxed{}\;\boxed{} \end{array}$$

Lee added the tens before the ones.

Circle the answers she got wrong.

$$\begin{array}{r} \boxed{} \\ 1\;\;1 \\ +\;5\;\;8 \\ \hline \boxed{6}\;\boxed{9} \end{array} \qquad \begin{array}{r} \boxed{1} \\ 1\;\;7 \\ +\;2\;\;7 \\ \hline \boxed{3}\;\boxed{4} \end{array} \qquad \begin{array}{r} \boxed{1} \\ 2\;\;6 \\ +\;2\;\;6 \\ \hline \boxed{4}\;\boxed{2} \end{array} \qquad \begin{array}{r} \boxed{} \\ 4\;\;3 \\ +\;2\;\;5 \\ \hline \boxed{6}\;\boxed{8} \end{array}$$

$29 + 14 \qquad\qquad 37 + 46 \qquad\qquad 48 + 23 \qquad\qquad 55 + 39$

Doubles

☐ Draw the same number of dots on the other side.
☐ Write a doubles sentence.

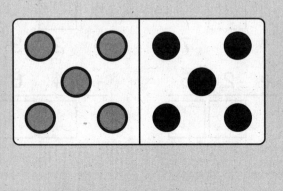

_**10**_ is double __**5**__

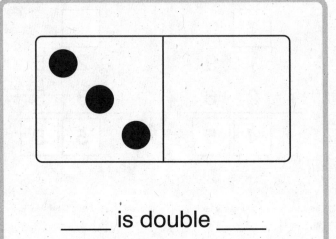

____ is double ____

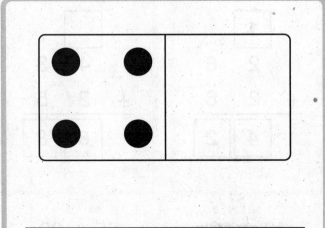

____ is double ____

____ is double ____

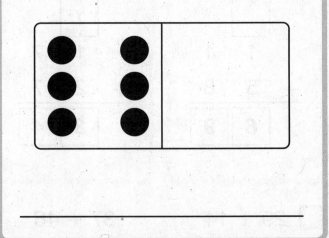

_____

_____

☐ Find the double.

The double of 5 + 3 = 8

● ● ● ● ● ○ ○ ○
● ● ● ● ● ○ ○ ○

is __10__ + __6__ = __16__

The double of 5 + 2 = 7

● ● ● ● ● ○ ○
● ● ● ● ● ○ ○

is ____ + ____ = ____

☐ Draw your own model to find the double.

The double of 5 + ____ = 9

is ____ + ____ = ____

The double of 5 + ____ = 10

is ____ + ____ = ____

☐ Now find the double without a model.

The double of 5 + ____ = 6

is ____ + ____ = ____

Using Doubles to Add

☐ Double, then add 1.

$4 + 4 = \underline{\textbf{8}}$ so $4 + 5 = \underline{\textbf{9}}$	$3 + 3 = \underline{}$ so $4 + 3 = \underline{}$
$7 + 7 = \underline{}$ so $8 + 7 = \underline{}$	$8 + 8 = \underline{}$ so $8 + 9 = \underline{}$
$6 + 6 = \underline{}$ so $6 + 7 = \underline{}$	$5 + 5 = \underline{}$ so $6 + 5 = \underline{}$
$\underline{} + \underline{} = \underline{}$ so $\quad 7 + 8 = \underline{}$	$\underline{} + \underline{} = \underline{}$ so $\quad 5 + 4 = \underline{}$
$\underline{} + \underline{} = \underline{}$ so $\quad 5 + 6 = \underline{}$	$\underline{} + \underline{} = \underline{}$ so $\quad 10 + 9 = \underline{}$

Bonus: Find $32 + 33$.

☐ Double, then subtract 1.

$7 + 7 = \underline{\textbf{14}}$
so $7 + 6 = \underline{\textbf{13}}$

$9 + 9 = \underline{}$
so $8 + 9 = \underline{}$

$6 + 6 = \underline{}$
so $6 + 5 = \underline{}$

$8 + 8 = \underline{}$
so $7 + 8 = \underline{}$

$8 + 8 = \underline{}$
so $8 + 7 = \underline{}$

$5 + 5 = \underline{}$
so $4 + 5 = \underline{}$

$\underline{} + \underline{} = \underline{}$
so $\quad 9 + 10 = \underline{}$

$\underline{} + \underline{} = \underline{}$
so $\quad 9 + 8 = \underline{}$

$\underline{} + \underline{} = \underline{}$
so $\quad 3 + 4 = \underline{}$

$\underline{} + \underline{} = \underline{}$
so $\quad 7 + 8 = \underline{}$

Bonus: Find $24 + 23$.

☐ Write how many **more** or **less**.
☐ Find the double.
☐ Add.

4 + 5 is _____**1 more than**_____ 4 + 4

4 + 4 = __8__ so 4 + 5 = __9__

---

7 + 9 is _____ 9 + 9

9 + 9 = ____ so 7 + 9 = ____

---

6 + 8 is _____ 8 + 8

8 + 8 = ____ so 6 + 8 = ____

---

6 + 7 is _____ 7 + 7

7 + 7 = ____ so 6 + 7 = ____

---

8 + 10 is _____ 10 + 10

10 + 10 = ____ so 8 + 10 = ____

---

7 + 6 is _____

_____ so 7 + 6 = ____

☐ Which two questions have the same answer?
Why did that happen?

☐ Write how many **more** or **less**, or **the same as**.
☐ Find the double.
☐ Add.

9 + 11 is _____*the same as*_____ 10 + 10

10 + 10 = __20__ so 9 + 11 = __20__

9 + 7 is _____ 8 + 8

8 + 8 = ____ so 9 + 7 = ____

8 + 9 is _____ 9 + 9

9 + 9 = ____ so 8 + 9 = ____

4 + 8 is _____ 6 + 6

6 + 6 = ____ so 4 + 8 = ____

9 + 7 is _____ 7 + 7

7 + 7 = ____ so 9 + 7 = ____

Which question did you do in two ways? ____ + ____

Did you get the same answer both times? _____

☐ Explain how it can be useful to do the same question in two ways.

Subtraction Strategies

☐ Count backward to subtract.

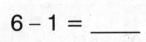

$6 - 1 = $ _____

$7 - 2 = $ _____

$8 - 3 = $ _____

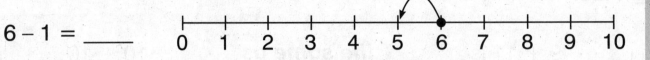

☐ Count forward to subtract.

$8 - 5 = $ _____

$9 - 6 = $ _____

$10 - 7 = $ _____

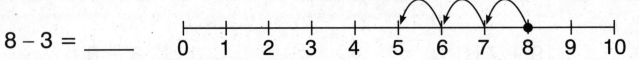

☐ Take away the coloured circles to subtract.

$10 - 2 = $ _____

$11 - 3 = $ _____

$12 - 4 = $ _____

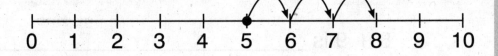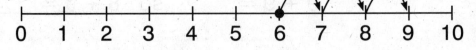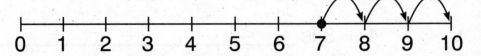

☐ Write 4 more subtraction sentences with the same answer.

_____ $10 - 6 = 4$ _____

_____   _____

☐ Circle the easiest problem to solve.

17 − 9	18 − 10	19 − 11	20 − 12

11 − 8	12 − 9	13 − 10	14 − 11

18 − 13	17 − 12	16 − 11	15 − 10

Explain your choices. _____

_____

☐ Make an easier problem with the same answer.
☐ Subtract.

$13 − 8 = \boxed{15} − 10 = \underline{\quad 5 \quad}$

$13 − 9 = \boxed{} − 10 = \underline{\qquad}$

$16 − 9 = \boxed{} − 10 = \underline{\qquad}$

$14 − 7 = \boxed{} − 10 = \underline{\qquad}$

$17 − 8 = \boxed{} − 10 = \underline{\qquad}$

$15 − 7 = \boxed{} − 10 = \underline{\qquad}$

$12 − 6 = \boxed{} − 10 = \underline{\qquad}$

Bonus

$24 − 18 = \boxed{} − 20 = \underline{\qquad}$

$13 - 3 =$ _____

10 11 12 13 14 15 16 17 18 19 20

$23 - 3 =$ _____

20 21 22 23 24 25 26 27 28 29 30

$33 - 3 =$ _____

30 31 32 33 34 35 36 37 38 39 40

$43 - 3 =$ _____

$73 - 3 =$ _____

$63 - 3 =$ _____

$93 - 3 =$ _____

$53 - 3 =$ _____

$83 - 3 =$ _____

$82 - 2 =$ _____

$67 - 7 =$ _____

$54 - 4 =$ _____

$91 - 1 =$ _____

$85 - 5 =$ _____

$76 - 6 =$ _____

$89 - 9 =$ _____

$50 - 0 =$ _____

$28 - 8 =$ _____

$74 - 4 =$ _____

$68 - 8 =$ _____

$41 - 1 =$ _____

Write how many more or less.
Subtract.

74 − 3 is _____**1 more than**_____ 73 − 3

73 − 3 = __70__   so   74 − 3 = __71__

83 − 5 is _____**2 less than**_____ 85 − 5

85 − 5 = ____   so   83 − 5 = ____

74 − 6 is _____ 76 − 6

76 − 6 = ____   so   74 − 6 = ____

57 − 6 is _____ 56 − 6

56 − 6 = ____   so   57 − 6 = ____

46 − 9 is _____ 49 − 9

49 − 9 = ____   so   46 − 9 = ____

Solve 75 − 8 in two ways.
Bonus: Solve 75 − 8 in a third way.

More Subtraction Strategies

☐ Count on to subtract.

36   37   38   39   40

$36 + \underline{\;4\;} = 40$ so $40 - 36 = \underline{\;4\;}$

$6 + \underline{} = 10$ so $10 - 6 = \underline{}$

$16 + \underline{} = 20$ so $20 - 16 = \underline{}$

$26 + \underline{} = 30$ so $30 - 26 = \underline{}$

$7 + \underline{} = 10$ so $10 - 7 = \underline{}$

$17 + \underline{} = 20$ so $20 - 17 = \underline{}$

$27 + \underline{} = 30$ so $30 - 27 = \underline{}$

$10 - 8 = \underline{}$

$20 - 18 = \underline{}$

$30 - 28 = \underline{}$

$10 - 5 = \underline{}$

$20 - 15 = \underline{}$

$30 - 25 = \underline{}$

$10 - 9 = \underline{}$

$40 - 39 = \underline{}$

$90 - 89 = \underline{}$

---

4   5   6   7   40   50   60   70

$7 - 4 = 3$ so $70 - 40 = 3$ tens $= 30$

$8 - 3 = \underline{\;5\;}$ so $80 - 30 = \underline{\;50\;}$

$7 - 2 = \underline{}$ so $70 - 20 = \underline{}$

$8 - 6 = \underline{}$ so $80 - 60 = \underline{}$

$10 - 5 = \underline{}$ so $100 - 50 = \underline{}$

$80 - 50 = \underline{}$

$70 - 30 = \underline{}$

$90 - 40 = \underline{}$

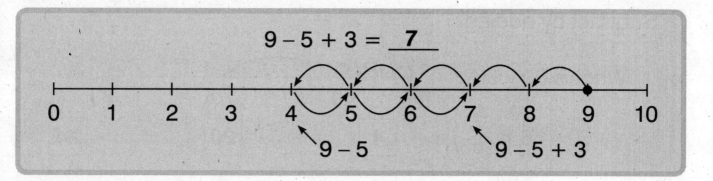

$9 - 5 + 3 = \underline{\textbf{7}}$

$6 - 2 + 3 = \underline{\hspace{1cm}}$

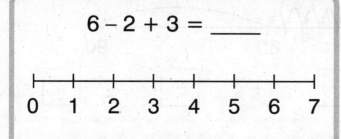

$7 - 4 + 3 = \underline{\hspace{1cm}}$

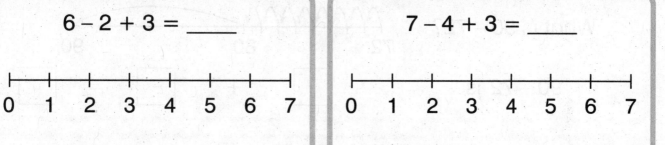

$4 + 3 - 3 = \underline{\hspace{1cm}}$

$5 + 2 - 2 = \underline{\hspace{1cm}}$

$7 - 5 + 5 = \underline{\hspace{1cm}}$

$6 - 4 + 4 = \underline{\hspace{1cm}}$

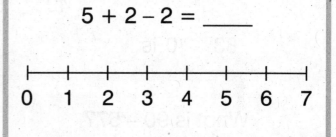

$7 + 6 - 6 = \underline{\hspace{1cm}}$

$8 - 4 + 4 = \underline{\hspace{1cm}}$

$10 - 3 + 3 = \underline{\hspace{1cm}}$

$14 - 10 + 10 = \underline{\hspace{1cm}}$

$31 + 8 - 8 = \underline{\hspace{1cm}}$

$27 + 15 - 15 = \underline{\hspace{1cm}}$

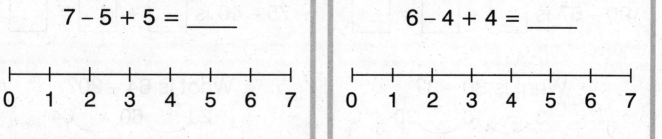

Number Sense 2-61

☐ Subtract by adding.

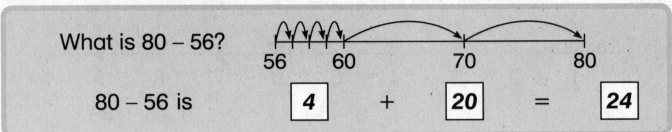

What is 80 − 56?

56   60   70   80

80 − 56 is   **4**   +   **20**   =   **24**

What is 90 − 72?

72   80   90

90 − 72 is   ☐   +   ☐   =   ☐

What is 83 − 40?

40   50   60   70   80 83

83 − 40 is   ☐   +   ☐ = ☐

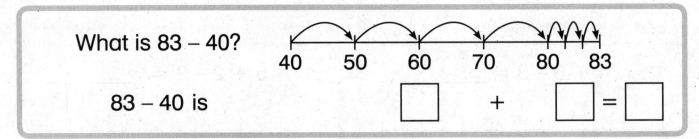

What is 90 − 57?

57   60   90

90 − 57 is ☐ + ☐ = ☐

What is 75 − 40?

40   70   75

75 − 40 is ☐ + ☐ = ☐

What is 30 − 3?

3   10   30

30 − 3 is ☐ + ☐ = ☐

What is 64 − 20?

20   60   64

64 − 20 is ☐ + ☐ = ☐

What is 77 − 40?

40   70   77

77 − 40 is ☐ + ☐ = ☐

What is 80 − 16?

16   20   80

80 − 16 is ☐ + ☐ = ☐

Subtract by using tens and adding.

$15 - 7 = \boxed{8}$

$7 \smile 10 \smile 15$

$\boxed{3} + \boxed{5} = \boxed{8}$

$25 - 17 = \boxed{}$

$17 \smile 20 \smile 25$

$\boxed{} + \boxed{} = \boxed{}$

$35 - 27 = \boxed{}$

$27 \smile 30 \smile 35$

$\boxed{} + \boxed{} = \boxed{}$

$42 - 36 = \boxed{}$

$36 \smile 40 \smile 42$

$\boxed{} + \boxed{} = \boxed{}$

$83 - 56 = \boxed{27}$

$56 \smile 60 \smile 80 \smile 83$

$\boxed{4} + \boxed{20} + \boxed{3} = \boxed{27}$

$92 - 49 = \boxed{}$

$49 \smile 50 \smile 90 \smile 92$

$\boxed{} + \boxed{} + \boxed{} = \boxed{}$

$78 - 29 = \boxed{}$

$29 \smile 30 \smile 70 \smile 78$

$\boxed{} + \boxed{} + \boxed{} = \boxed{}$

$95 - 57 = \boxed{}$

$57 \smile 60 \smile 90 \smile 95$

$\boxed{} + \boxed{} + \boxed{} = \boxed{}$

☐ Subtract by adding in different ways.

12 − 7 = ⬚5⬚ 7 ⌣ 8 ⌣ 12
⬚1⬚ + ⬚4⬚

12 − 7 = ☐ 7 ⌣ 9 ⌣ 12
☐ + ☐

12 − 7 = ☐ 7 ⌣ 10 ⌣ 12
☐ + ☐

13 − 6 = ☐ 6 ⌣ 12 ⌣ 13
☐ + ☐

13 − 6 = ☐ 6 ⌣ 10 ⌣ 13
☐ + ☐

13 − 6 = ☐ 6 ⌣ 8 ⌣ 13
☐ + ☐

60 − 24 = ☐ 24 ⌣ 30 ⌣ 60
☐ + ☐

60 − 24 = ☐ 24 ⌣ 54 ⌣ 60
☐ + ☐

60 − 24 = ☐ 24 ⌣ 50 ⌣ 60
☐ + ☐

43 − 18 = ☐ 18 ⌣ 20 ⌣ 40 ⌣ 43
☐ + ☐ + ☐

43 − 18 = ☐ 18 ⌣ 20 ⌣ 23 ⌣ 43
☐ + ☐ + ☐

43 − 18 = ☐ 18 ⌣ 29 ⌣ 36 ⌣ 43
☐ + ☐ + ☐

☐ Circle the easiest way to do each problem above.

Explain one choice. _____

_____

Subtracting Using Tens and Ones

☐ Use ones blocks and tens blocks to subtract.
☐ Colour blocks to show the second number.
   What number do the **white** blocks show?

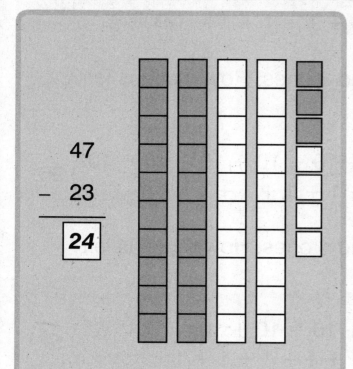

47
− 23
___
24

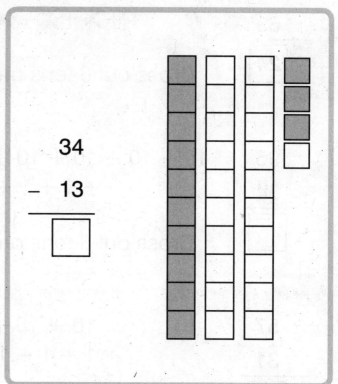

34
− 13
___
☐

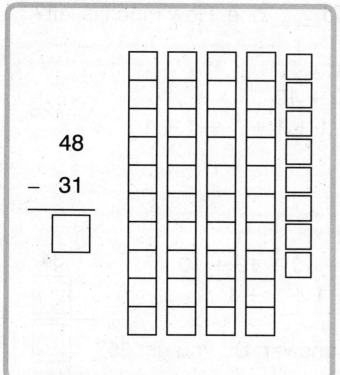

48
− 31
___
☐

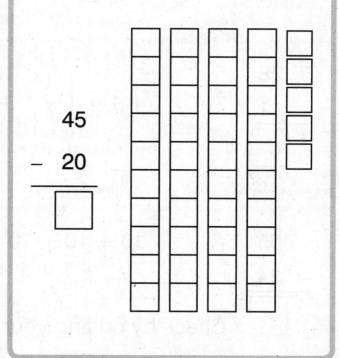

45
− 20
___
☐

☐ Cross out the correct number of 10s and 1s.
☐ Subtract.

87
− 63
24

⮽ + ⮽ + ⮽ + ⮽ + ⮽ + ⮽ + 10 + 10
+ ✗ + ✗ + ✗ + 1 + 1 + 1 + 1 ⎞ 87

Cross out 6 tens and 3 ones. How much is left?

96
− 34
☐

10 + 10 + 10 + 10 + 10 + 10 + 10 + 10 + 10 ⎞ 96
+ 1 + 1 + 1 + 1 + 1 + 1

Cross out 3 tens and 4 ones. How much is left?

57
− 31
☐

10 + 10 + 10 + 10 + 10 ⎞ 57
+ 1 + 1 + 1 + 1 + 1 + 1 + 1

Cross out ____ tens and ____ one. How much is left?

28
− 11
☐

10 + 10 ⎞ 28
+ 1 + 1 + 1 + 1 + 1 + 1 + 1 + 1

65
− 34
☐

10 + 10 + 10 + 10 + 10 + 10
+ 1 + 1 + 1 + 1 + 1

34
+ ☐
☐

Check by adding your answer. Do you get 65?

☐ Subtract.

8	5
− 4	2
4	**3**

8 tens 5 ones
− 4 tens 2 ones
4 tens **3** ones

6	7
− 2	5

6 tens 7 ones
− 2 tens 5 ones
☐ tens ☐ ones

9	7
− 2	1

9 tens 7 ones
− 2 tens 1 ones
☐ tens ☐ ones

6	3
− 4	2

6 tens 3 ones
− 4 tens 2 ones
☐ tens ☐ ones

☐ Subtract, then check your answer by adding.

tens	ones
6	9
− 5	3

check
5	3
+	

tens	ones
8	5
− 3	1

check
3	1
+	

tens	ones
7	8
− 3	7

check
+	

tens	ones
6	9
− 2	4

check
+	

Regrouping for Subtraction

To find 45 – 28, Miki draws tens and ones blocks for 45. She tries to colour 28.

Miki can only colour 25, so she trades a tens block for 10 ones blocks. Now Miki can colour 28.

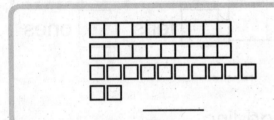

45 – 28 = 17
There are 17 left.

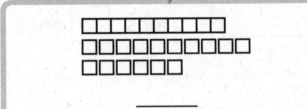

What number is shown?

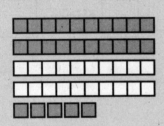

_____

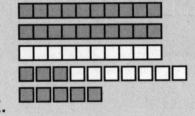

_____

☐ Write the subtraction sentence for the model.

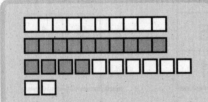

32 – **14** = **18**

____ – ____ = ____

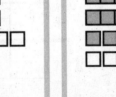

____ – ____ = ____

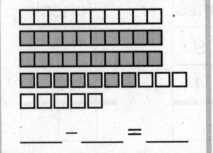

____ – ____ = ____

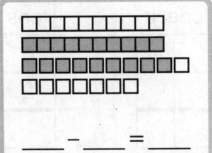

____ – ____ = ____

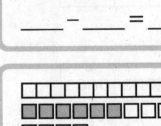

____ – ____ = ____

☐ Show Miki's trade in a tens and ones chart.

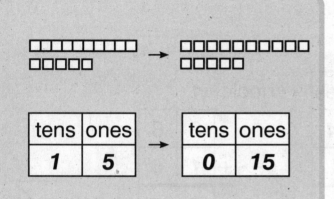

tens	ones
1	5

→

tens	ones
0	15

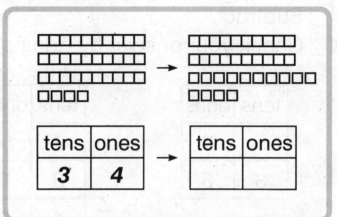

tens	ones
3	4

→

tens	ones

☐ Show Miki's subtraction using a tens and ones chart.

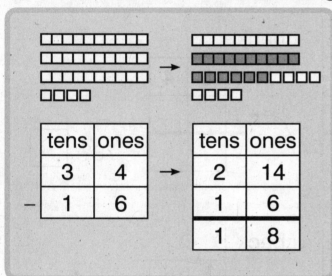

tens	ones
3	4
− 1	6

→

tens	ones
2	14
1	6
1	8

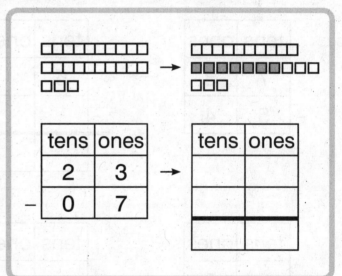

tens	ones
2	3
− 0	7

→

tens	ones

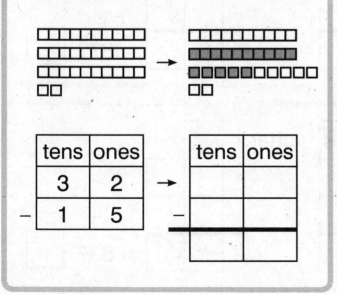

tens	ones
3	2
− 1	5

→

tens	ones
−	

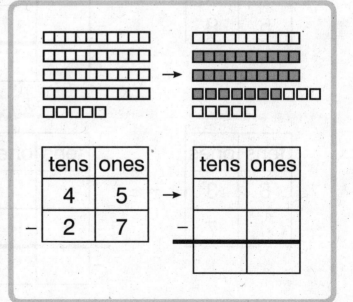

tens	ones
4	5
− 2	7

→

tens	ones
−	

☐ Trade a ten for 10 ones.
☐ Subtract.
☐ Check your answer by adding.

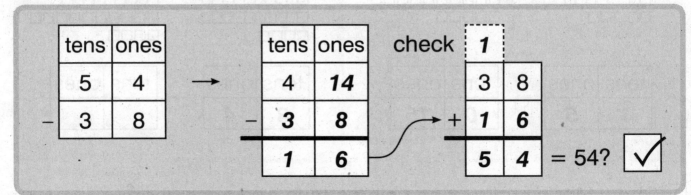

tens	ones
5	4
− 3	8

→

tens	ones
4	14
− 3	8
1	6

check

	1
3	8
+ 1	6
5	4

= 54? ✓

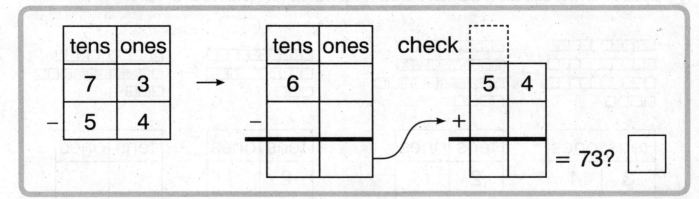

tens	ones
7	3
− 5	4

→

tens	ones
6	
−	

check

5	4
+	

= 73? ☐

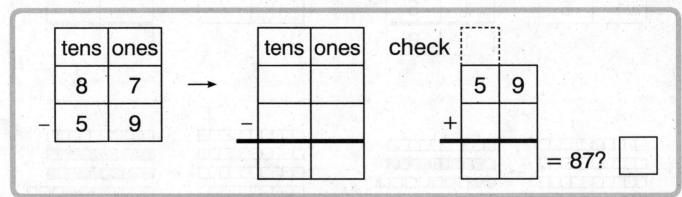

tens	ones
8	7
− 5	9

→

tens	ones
−	

check

5	9
+	

= 87? ☐

tens	ones
6	3
− 4	7

→

tens	ones
−	

check

+	

= 63? ☐

The Standard Algorithm for Subtraction

◻ Take 1 ten from the tens and add 10 ones to the ones.
◻ Use standard notation.

50 = __5__ tens + __0__ ones

= __4__ tens + __10__ ones

4	10
5̸	0̸

73 = __7__ tens + __3__ ones

= ____ tens + ____ ones

7	3

85 = ____ tens + ____ ones

= ____ tens + ____ ones

8	5

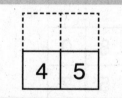

5	11
6̸	1̸

7	7

8	6

4	2

3	9

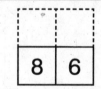

1	6

2	3

7	1

4	5

5	4

3	0

3	2

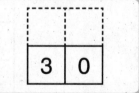

6	8

5	5

2	9

9	0

Subtract using the standard algorithm.

$$
\begin{array}{r}
{\scriptstyle 6}\ {\scriptstyle 15} \\
\not{7}\ \not{5} \\
-\ 5\ 7 \\
\hline
1\ 8
\end{array}
$$

$$
\begin{array}{r}
8\ 3 \\
-\ 5\ 6 \\
\hline
\end{array}
$$

$$
\begin{array}{r}
5\ 4 \\
-\ 3\ 9 \\
\hline
\end{array}
$$

$$
\begin{array}{r}
4\ 6 \\
-\ 2\ 7 \\
\hline
\end{array}
$$

$$
\begin{array}{r}
9\ 2 \\
-\ 8\ 7 \\
\hline
\end{array}
$$

$$
\begin{array}{r}
8\ 1 \\
-\ 5\ 5 \\
\hline
\end{array}
$$

$$
\begin{array}{r}
5\ 3 \\
-\ 2\ 9 \\
\hline
\end{array}
$$

$$
\begin{array}{r}
6\ 0 \\
-\ 3\ 6 \\
\hline
\end{array}
$$

$$
\begin{array}{r}
9\ 1 \\
-\ 7\ 2 \\
\hline
\end{array}
$$

$$
\begin{array}{r}
9\ 6 \\
-\ 2\ 9 \\
\hline
\end{array}
$$

$$
\begin{array}{r}
8\ 7 \\
-\ 3\ 8 \\
\hline
\end{array}
$$

$$
\begin{array}{r}
8\ 0 \\
-\ 5\ 7 \\
\hline
\end{array}
$$

Check your answers by adding.

☐ Decide if you need to regroup. Subtract.

	4	8
−	2	5

	4	7
−	1	9

	4	9
−	1	7

	5	3
−	4	8

	5	8
−	4	3

	6	7
−	3	3

	5	8
−	2	6

	7	0
−	3	7

	8	1
−	6	1

	9	8
−	2	7

	8	5
−	3	6

	9	0
−	4	8

▱ Check your answers by adding.

☐ Subtract in two ways.

standard	by adding
$\begin{array}{cc} 8 & 5 \\ - \ 3 & 3 \\ \hline & \end{array}$	33 40 80 85 ☐ + ☐ + ☐ = ☐
$\begin{array}{cc} 7 & 2 \\ - \ 5 & 6 \\ \hline & \end{array}$	56 60 70 72 ☐ + ☐ + ☐ = ☐
$\begin{array}{cc} 9 & 6 \\ - \ 4 & 9 \\ \hline & \end{array}$	49 50 90 96 ☐ + ☐ + ☐ = ☐
$\begin{array}{cc} 6 & 8 \\ - \ 4 & 3 \\ \hline & \end{array}$	43 50 60 68 ☐ + ☐ + ☐ = ☐

☐ Subtract by adding to find 72 − 13.
Who is right? Explain what the others did wrong.

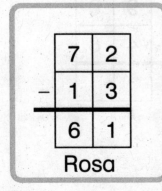

Rosa	Bob	Sam	Lina
$\begin{array}{cc} 7 & 2 \\ - \ 1 & 3 \\ \hline 6 & 1 \end{array}$	$\begin{array}{cc} 7 & 2 \\ - \ 1 & 3 \\ \hline 6 & 5 \end{array}$	$\begin{array}{cc} & 12 \\ 7 & \not{2} \\ - \ 1 & 3 \\ \hline 6 & 9 \end{array}$	$\begin{array}{cc} 6 & 12 \\ \not{7} & \not{2} \\ - \ 1 & 3 \\ \hline 5 & 9 \end{array}$

Three-Digit Numbers

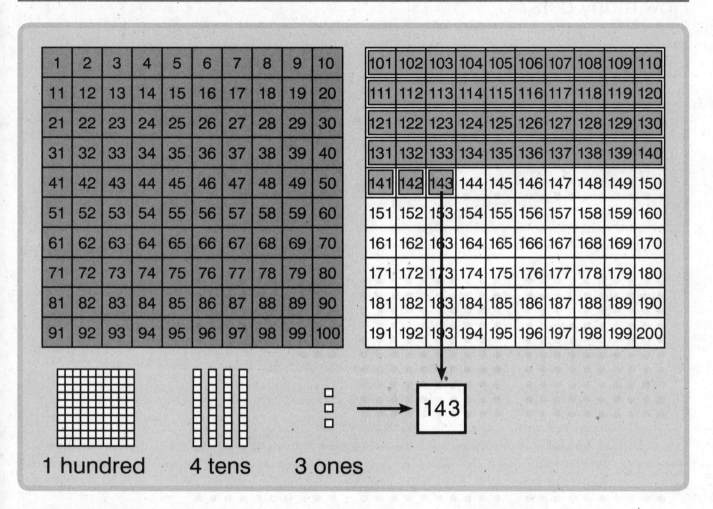

1 hundred   4 tens   3 ones

What number does each set show?

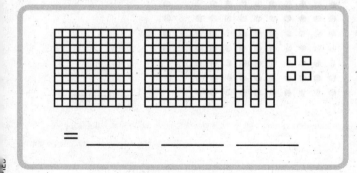

= _____ _____ _____

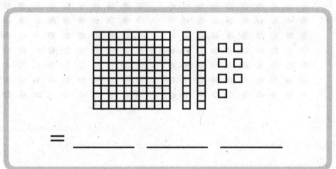

= _____ _____ _____

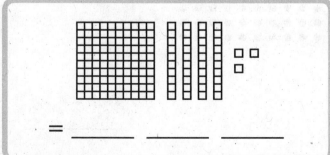

= _____ _____ _____

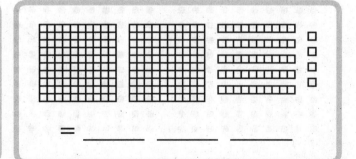

= _____ _____ _____

How many dots?

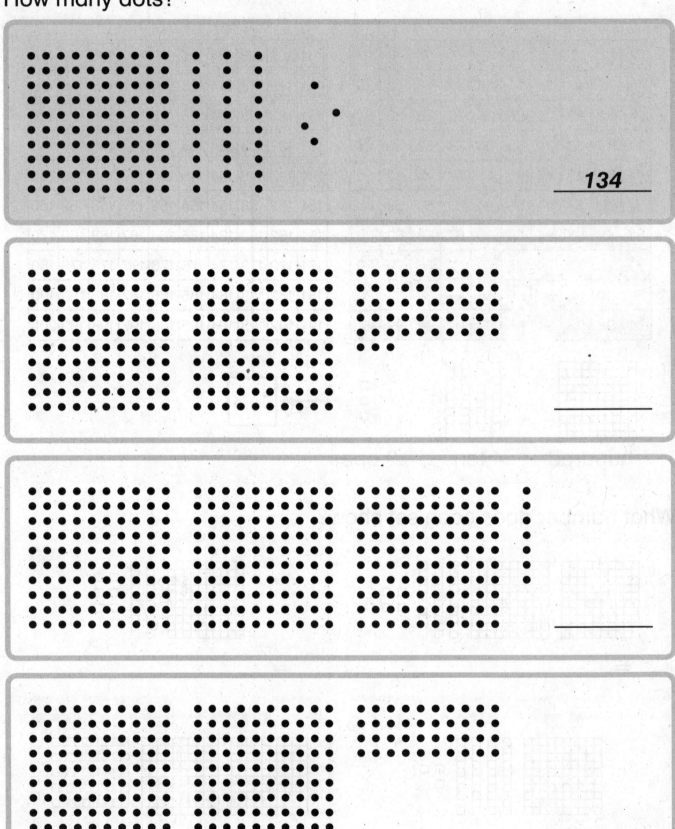

134

Use hundreds, tens, and ones blocks to make each number.
Write the number you made.

1	2	3	4	5	6	7	8	9	10
11	12	13	14	15	16	17	18	19	20
21	22	23	24	25	26	27	28	29	30
31	32	33	34	35	36	37	38	39	40
41	42	43	44	45	46	47	48	49	50
51	52	53	54	55	56	57	58	59	60
61	62	63	64	65	66	67	68	69	70
71	72	73	74	75	76	77	78	79	80
81	82	83	84	85	86	87	88	89	90
91	92	93	94	95	96	97	98	99	100

101	102	103	104	105	106	107	108	109	110
111	112	113	114	115	116	117	118	119	120
121	122	123	124	125	126	127	128	129	130
131	132	133	134	135	136	137	138	139	140
141	142	143	144	145	146	147	148	149	150
151	152	153	154	155	156	157	158	159	160
161	162	163	164	165	166	167	168	169	170
171	172	173	174	175	176	177	178	179	180
181	182	183	184	185	186	187	188	189	190
191	192	193	194	195	196	197	198	199	200

1 hundred
4 tens
+ 3 ones
_____

14 tens
+ 3 ones
_____

13 tens
+ 13 ones
_____

12 tens
+ 23 ones
_____

A **ones** digit of 4 means: $4 = 1 + 1 + 1 + 1$

A **tens** digit of 5 means: $50 = 10 + 10 + 10 + 10 + 10$

A **hundreds** digit of 3 means: $300 = 100 + 100 + 100$

☐ Write the number as a sum of 100s, 10s, and 1s.

$324 = \mathbf{100 + 100 + 100 + 10 + 10 + 1 + 1 + 1 + 1}$

$213 =$

$320 =$

☐ We can write $324 = 300 + 20 + 4$. Write each number in this way.

$102 = \mathbf{100 + 2}$

$546 =$

$904 =$

$490 =$

☐ Add.

$400 + 70 = $ _____

$400 + 7 = $ _____

$300 + 50 = $ _____

$200 + 70 = $ _____

$60 + 100 = $ _____

$9 + 300 = $ _____

$30 + 2 + 400 = $ _____

$20 + 500 + 4 = $ _____

Bonus: $2000 + 300 + 7 = $ _____

☐ Add.

$$4 \qquad + \qquad 3$$
$$= 1 + 1 + 1 + 1 \qquad + \qquad 1 + 1 + 1 \qquad = \underline{\qquad}$$

$$40 \qquad + \qquad 30$$
$$= 10 + 10 + 10 + 10 \qquad + \qquad 10 + 10 + 10 \qquad = \underline{\qquad}$$

$$400 \qquad + \qquad 300$$
$$= 100 + 100 + 100 + 100 \qquad + \qquad 100 + 100 + 100 \qquad = \underline{\qquad}$$

$2 + 4 = \underline{\qquad}$

$20 + 40 = \underline{\qquad}$

$200 + 400 = \underline{\qquad}$

$3 + 2 = \underline{\qquad}$

$30 + 20 = \underline{\qquad}$

$300 + 200 = \underline{\qquad}$

$1 + 7 = \underline{\qquad}$

$10 + 70 = \underline{\qquad}$

$100 + 700 = \underline{\qquad}$

$5 + 4 = \underline{\qquad}$

$50 + 40 = \underline{\qquad}$

$500 + 400 = \underline{\qquad}$

$1 + 2 + 4 = \underline{\qquad}$

$10 + 20 + 40 = \underline{\qquad}$

$100 + 200 + 400 = \underline{\qquad}$

$2 + 2 + 5 = \underline{\qquad}$

$20 + 20 + 50 = \underline{\qquad}$

$200 + 200 + 500 = \underline{\qquad}$

Bonus: $60 + 2 + 100 + 4 + 20 + 400 = \underline{\qquad}$

Skip Counting to 200

☐ Start at 0.

☐ Finish shading the numbers you say when skip counting by 5s.

1	2	3	4	5	6	7	8	9	10
11	12	13	14	15	16	17	18	19	20
21	22	23	24	25	26	27	28	29	30
31	32	33	34	35	36	37	38	39	40
41	42	43	44	45	46	47	48	49	50
51	52	53	54	55	56	57	58	59	60
61	62	63	64	65	66	67	68	69	70
71	72	73	74	75	76	77	78	79	80
81	82	83	84	85	86	87	88	89	90
91	92	93	94	95	96	97	98	99	100

101	102	103	104	105	106	107	108	109	110
111	112	113	114	115	116	117	118	119	120
121	122	123	124	125	126	127	128	129	130
131	132	133	134	135	136	137	138	139	140
141	142	143	144	145	146	147	148	149	150
151	152	153	154	155	156	157	158	159	160
161	162	163	164	165	166	167	168	169	170
171	172	173	174	175	176	177	178	179	180
181	182	183	184	185	186	187	188	189	190
191	192	193	194	195	196	197	198	199	200

☐ Count by 5s.

85 _____ _____ _____ *110* _____

140 _____ _____ _____ _____ _____

☐ Count by 10s.

70 _____ _____ _____ _____ _____

☐ Count by 2s.

142 _____ _____ _____ _____ _____

⬚ Shade the numbers you say when counting by 25s.

1	2	3	4	5	6	7	8	9	10
11	12	13	14	15	16	17	18	19	20
21	22	23	24	25	26	27	28	29	30
31	32	33	34	35	36	37	38	39	40
41	42	43	44	45	46	47	48	49	50
51	52	53	54	55	56	57	58	59	60
61	62	63	64	65	66	67	68	69	70
71	72	73	74	75	76	77	78	79	80
81	82	83	84	85	86	87	88	89	90
91	92	93	94	95	96	97	98	99	100

101	102	103	104	105	106	107	108	109	110
111	112	113	114	115	116	117	118	119	120
121	122	123	124	125	126	127	128	129	130
131	132	133	134	135	136	137	138	139	140
141	142	143	144	145	146	147	148	149	150
151	152	153	154	155	156	157	158	159	160
161	162	163	164	165	166	167	168	169	170
171	172	173	174	175	176	177	178	179	180
181	182	183	184	185	186	187	188	189	190
191	192	193	194	195	196	197	198	199	200

⬚ Count by 25s from 0 to 200.

_0_   _25_   _____   _____   _____

         _125_   _____   _____   _____

How much money?

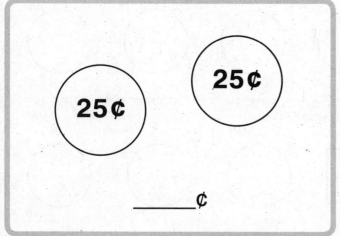

_____ ¢

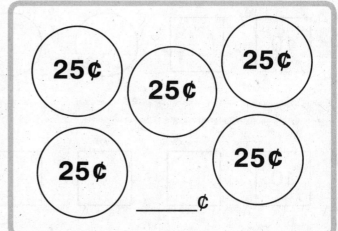

_____ ¢

Skip Counting by Different Numbers

☐ Skip count by ⬦5s⬦, then by ①s.

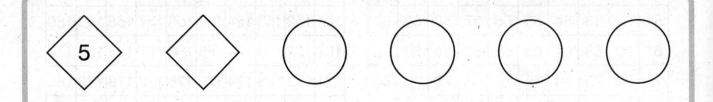

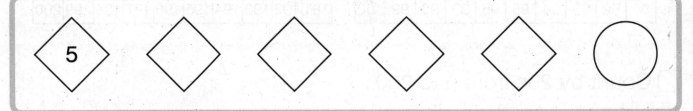

☐ Skip count by 10s, then by ①s.

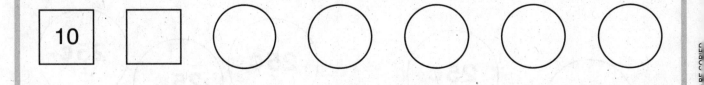

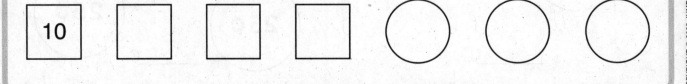

☐ Skip count by ⬜10s, then by ◇5s.

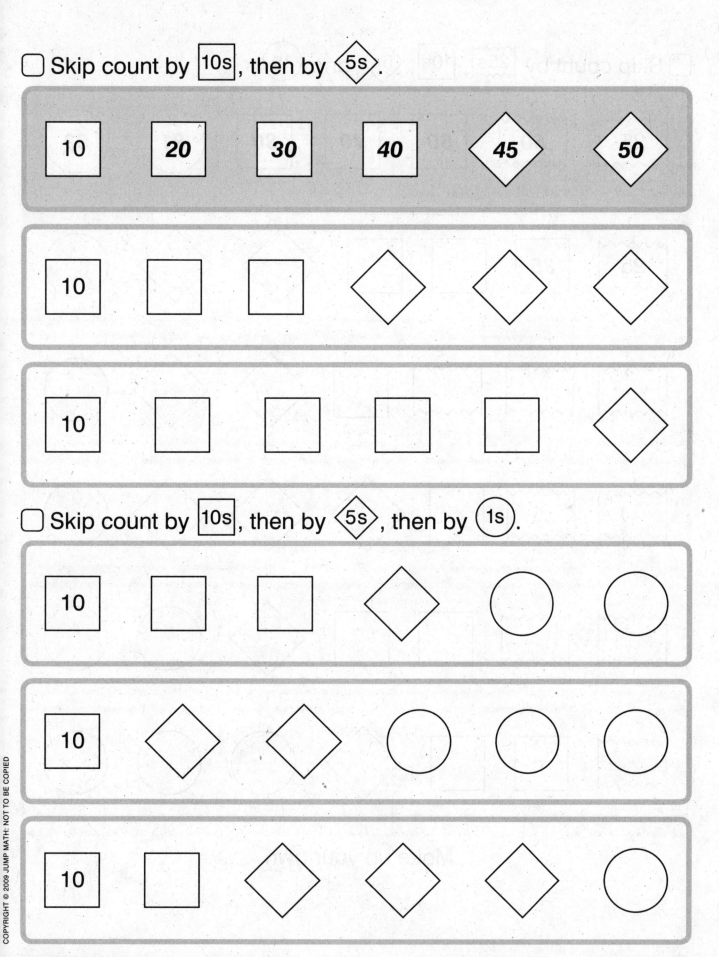

| 10 | 20 | 30 | 40 | 45 | 50 |

☐ Skip count by ⬜10s, then by ◇5s, then by ○1s.

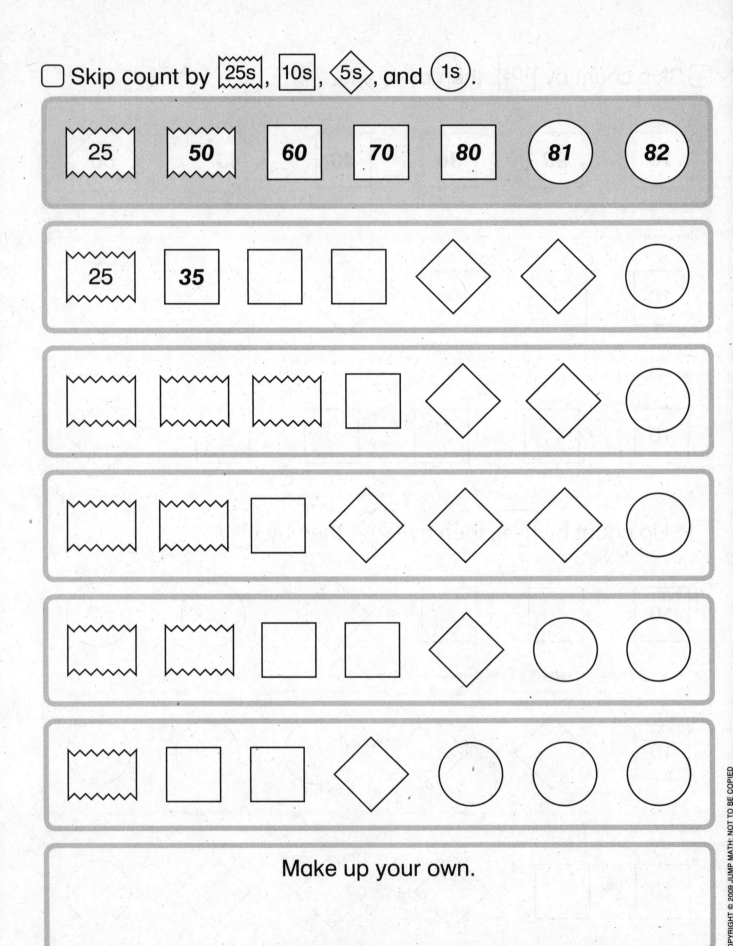

Skip count by 25s, 10s, 5s, and 1s.

| 25 | 50 | 60 | 70 | 80 | 81 | 82 |

| 25 | 35 | | | | | |

Make up your own.

Coin Values

☐ Write the value on the coin.
☐ Write the name of the coin.

| quarter | loonie | dime |
| nickel | ~~penny~~ | toonie |

_____**penny**_____

_____

_____

_____

_____

_____

Estimating and Counting Money

☐ Estimate how much money. _____ ¢

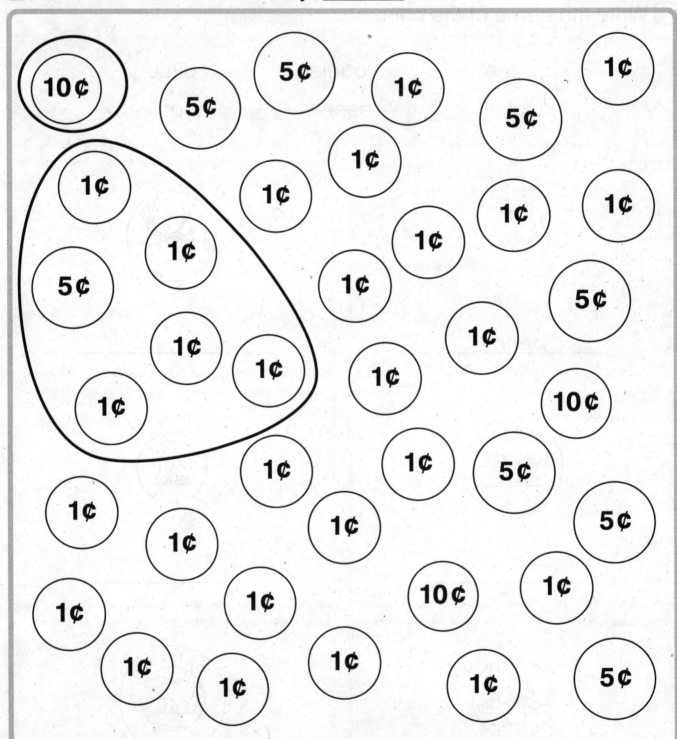

☐ Circle groups of 10 cents.
   How much money is there? _____

- ☐ Estimate how much money.
- ☐ Circle all groups of 25¢ using red.
- ☐ Then circle all groups of 10¢ using blue.
- ☐ Count the money.

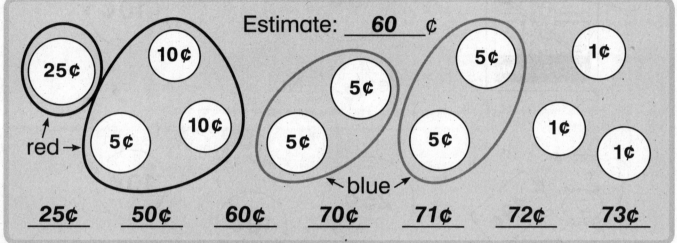

Estimate: __60__ ¢

red →

← blue →

| 25¢ | 50¢ | 60¢ | 70¢ | 71¢ | 72¢ | 73¢ |

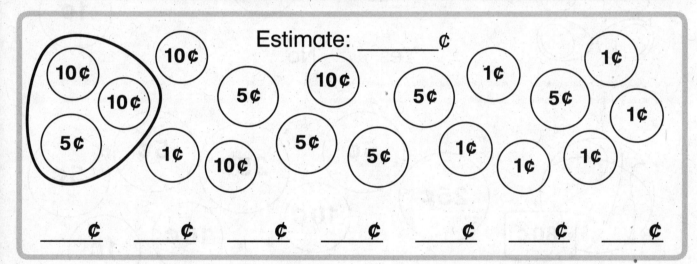

Estimate: _____ ¢

___¢ ___¢ ___¢ ___¢ ___¢ ___¢ ___¢

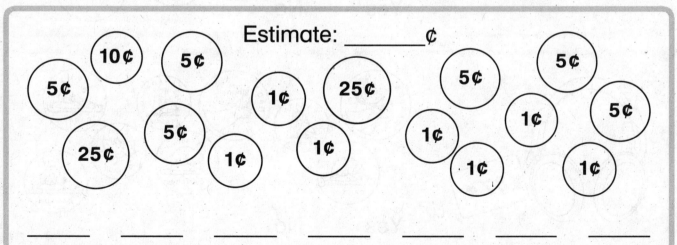

Estimate: _____ ¢

___ ___ ___ ___ ___

Does Lisa have enough money?

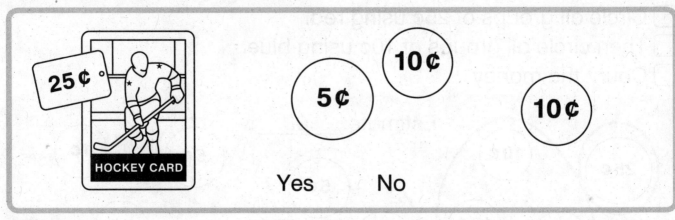

Yes   No

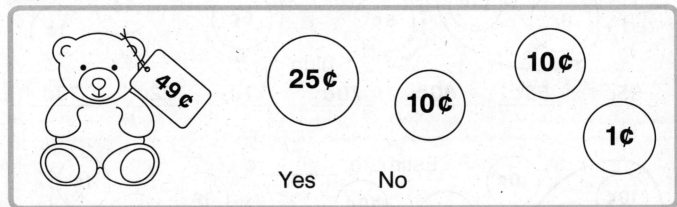

Yes   No

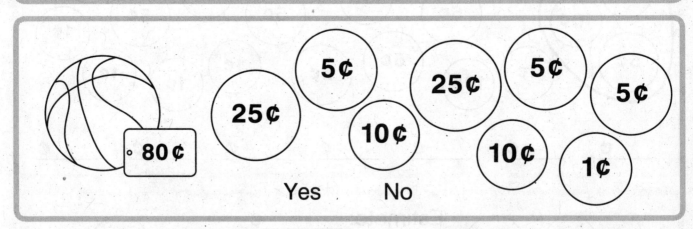

Yes   No

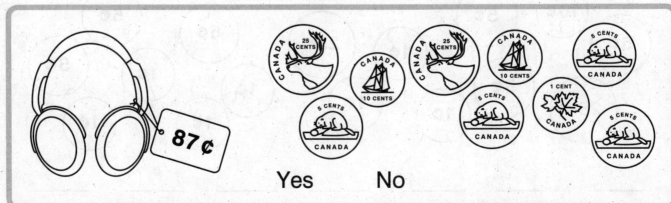

Yes   No

☐ Make 12¢ using…

3 coins	4 coins

☐ Make 27¢ using…

3 coins	5 coins

6 coins	7 coins

📓 Make each amount using the fewest coins.

8¢   15¢   21¢   31¢   36¢

📓 Show how many different ways you can make 12¢ using nickels and pennies.

Adding Money

☐ Mary adds coins to her bag.
How much money does she have now?

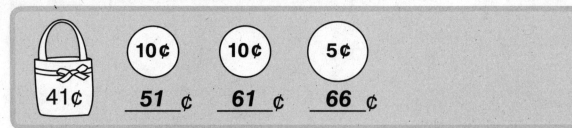

41¢   10¢   __51__ ¢   10¢   __61__ ¢   5¢   __66__ ¢

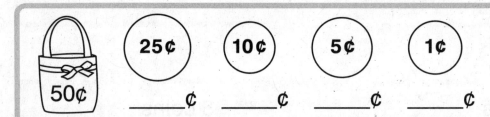

50¢   25¢   ____ ¢   10¢   ____ ¢   5¢   ____ ¢   1¢   ____ ¢

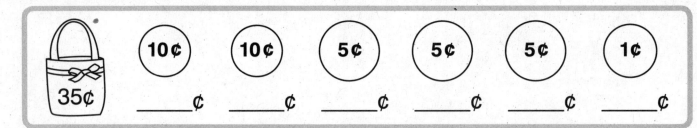

35¢   10¢   ____ ¢   10¢   ____ ¢   5¢   ____ ¢   5¢   ____ ¢   5¢   ____ ¢   1¢   ____ ¢

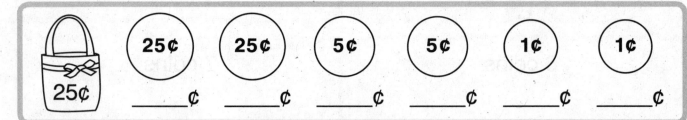

25¢   25¢   ____ ¢   25¢   ____ ¢   5¢   ____ ¢   5¢   ____ ¢   1¢   ____ ¢   1¢   ____ ¢

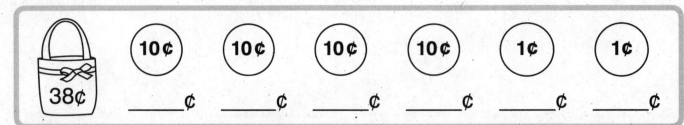

38¢   10¢   ____ ¢   10¢   ____ ¢   10¢   ____ ¢   10¢   ____ ¢   1¢   ____ ¢   1¢   ____ ¢

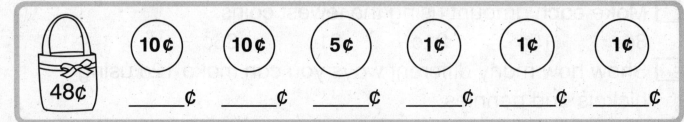

48¢   10¢   ____ ¢   10¢   ____ ¢   5¢   ____ ¢   1¢   ____ ¢   1¢   ____ ¢   1¢   ____ ¢

Bilal adds coins to his bag.
How much money does he have now?

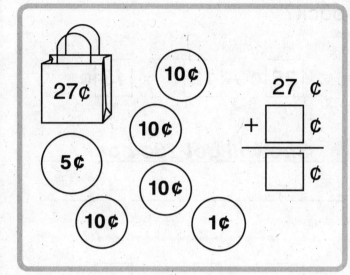

27 ¢
+ ☐ ¢
─────
☐ ¢

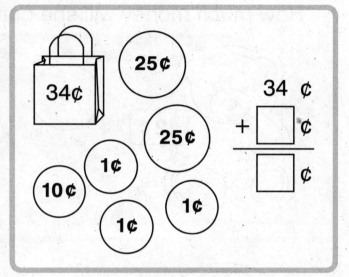

34 ¢
+ ☐ ¢
─────
☐ ¢

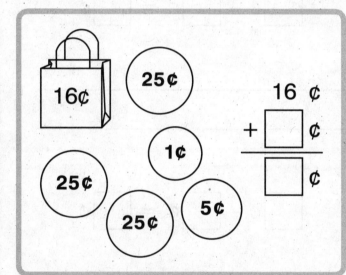

16 ¢
+ ☐ ¢
─────
☐ ¢

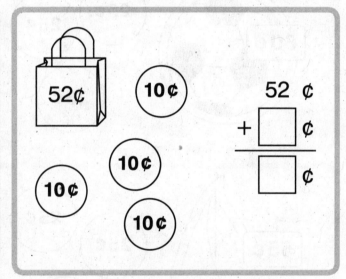

52 ¢
+ ☐ ¢
─────
☐ ¢

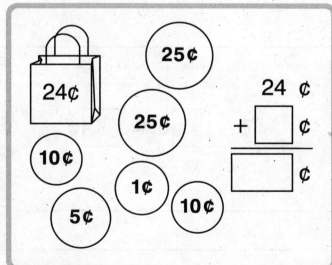

24 ¢
+ ☐ ¢
─────
☐ ¢

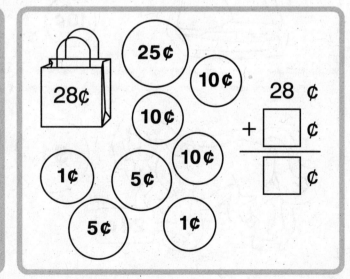

28 ¢
+ ☐ ¢
─────
☐ ¢

Subtracting Money

☐ Lisa pays for stickers.
How much money will she get back?

$$\boxed{25}\,¢ - \boxed{12}\,¢ = \boxed{13}\,¢$$

She will get 13¢ back.

_____

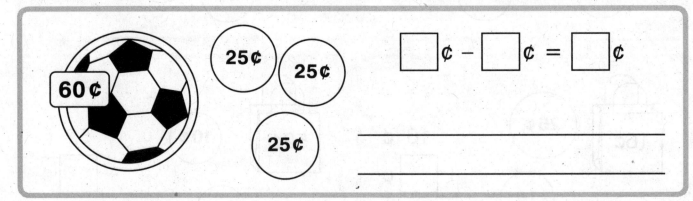

$$\boxed{}\,¢ - \boxed{}\,¢ = \boxed{}\,¢$$

_____

_____

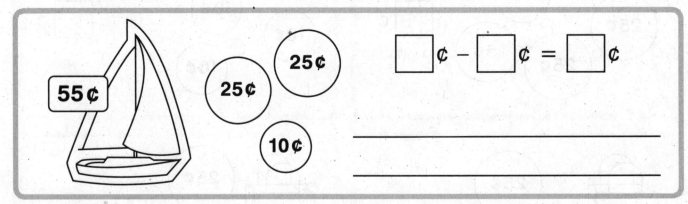

$$\boxed{}\,¢ - \boxed{}\,¢ = \boxed{}\,¢$$

_____

_____

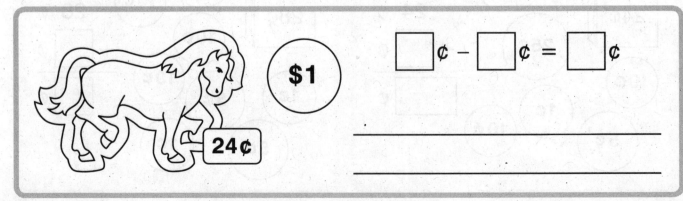

$$\boxed{}\,¢ - \boxed{}\,¢ = \boxed{}\,¢$$

_____

_____

☐ Write an addition or subtraction sentence.
☐ Solve the problem.

Rosa has 17¢.

She finds 3 dimes.

Rosa now has _____¢.

$$\begin{array}{r} \boxed{17} \\ + \boxed{30} \\ \hline \boxed{47} \end{array}$$

Miki has 60¢.

He gave his sister a quarter.

Miki has _____¢ left.

Daniel has 2 dimes and 3 nickels.

Ron has 2 quarters.

Ron has _____¢ more than Daniel.

Ahmed has 3 nickels and 7 pennies.

Lina has 2 dimes.

Ahmed and Lina have _____¢ altogether.

Fractions

☐ Write half, third, fourth, or fifth.

There are two equal parts.

Each part is a ___**half**___.

There are **th**ree equal parts.

Each part is a _____.

There are **four** equal parts.

Each part is a _____.

There are **five** equal parts.

Each part is a _____.

Each part is a _____.

Each part is a _____.

Each part is a _____.

Each part is a _____.

Each part is a _____.

Each part is a _____.

☐ Colour the fraction.

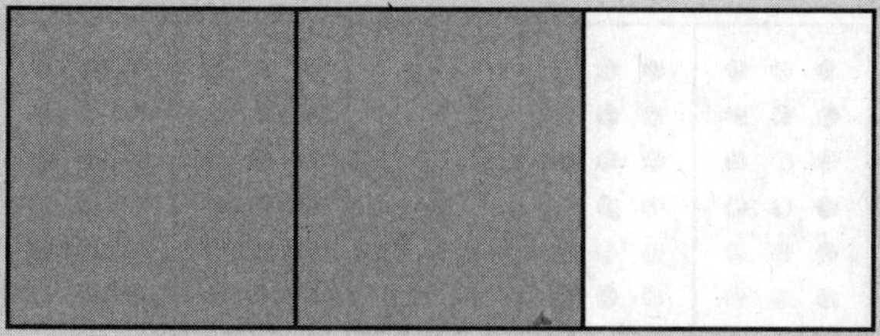

two thirds

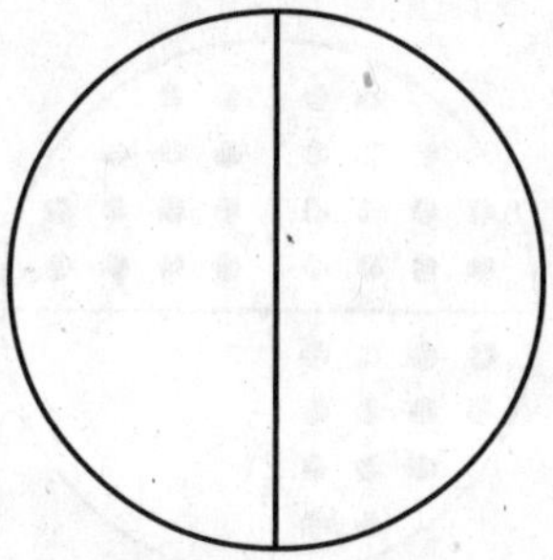

one half

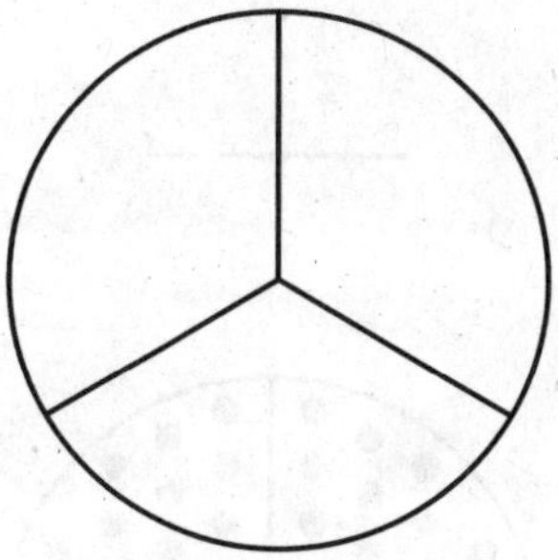

one third

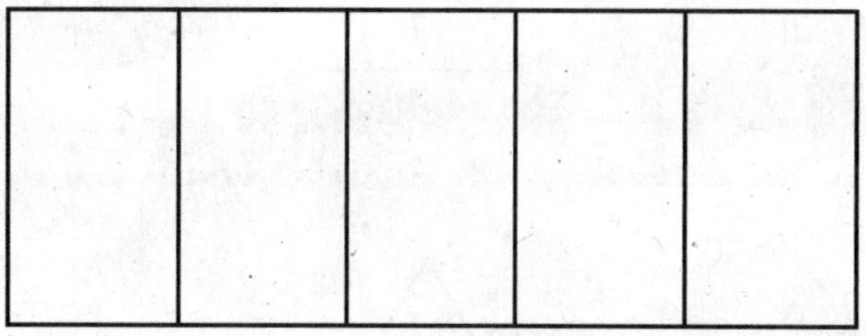

three fifths

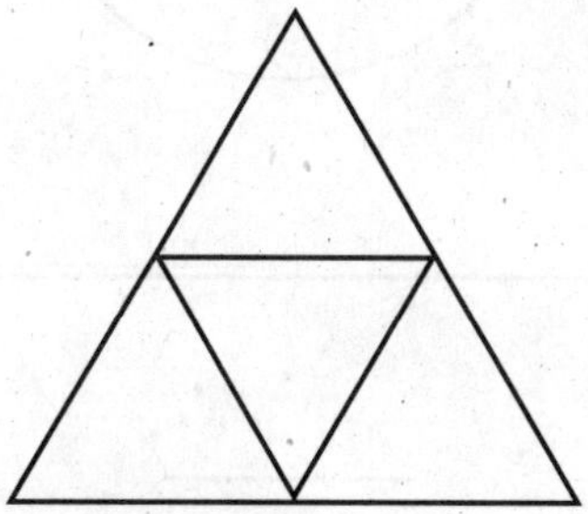

three fourths

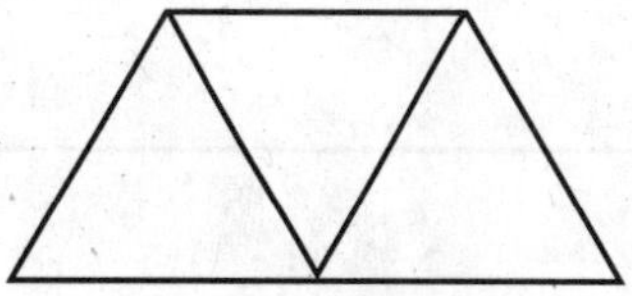

two thirds

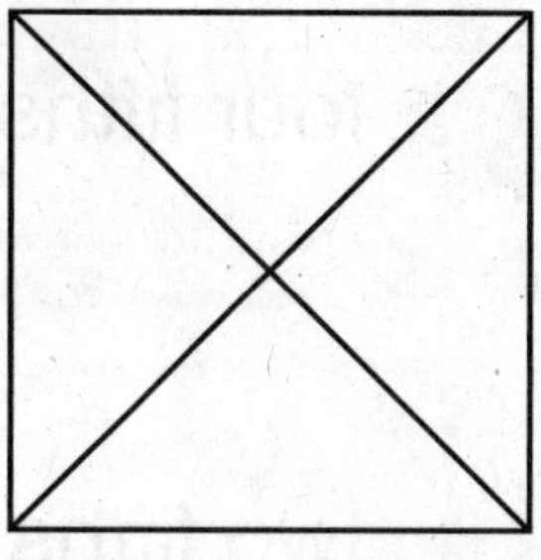

two fourths

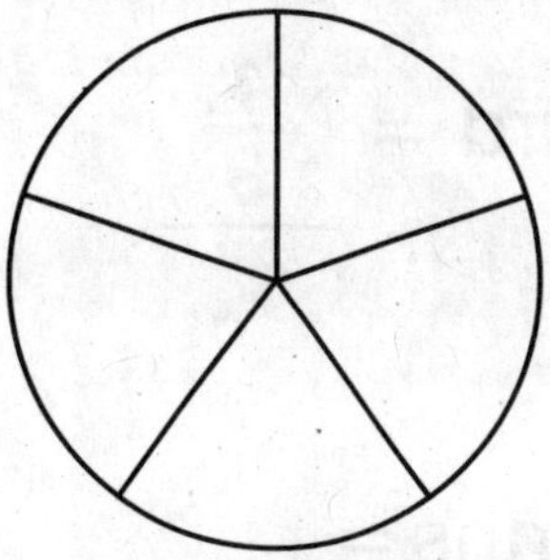

four fifths

□ What fraction is dotted? Write the fraction in two ways.

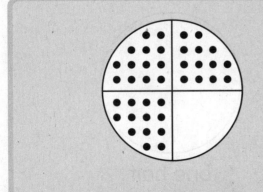

three fourths

$$\frac{3}{4}$$

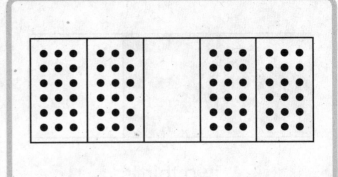

_____

____

_____

____

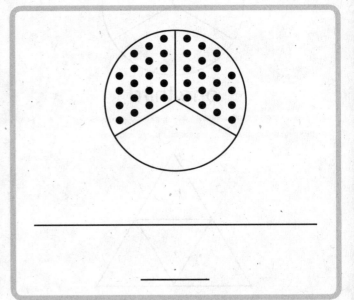

_____

____

□ Write the fraction.

one third = $\frac{1}{3}$

three fifths = ____

four fifths = ____

two fourths = ____

one half = ____

two fifths = ____

☐ ✓ what is true and ✗ what is not true.
Does the picture have $\frac{3}{4}$ shaded?

☑ 3 parts are shaded.
☑ There are 4 parts in total.
___no___ ☒ All parts are the same size.

☐ 3 parts are shaded.
☐ There are 4 parts in total.
_____ ☐ All parts are the same size.

☐ 3 parts are shaded.
☐ There are 4 parts in total.
_____ ☐ All parts are the same size.

☐ 3 parts are shaded.
☐ There are 4 parts in total.
_____ ☐ All parts are the same size.

☐ Does the picture ⬤ have $\frac{2}{5}$ shaded?
Explain how you know.

Comparing Fractions

Who ate more pizza?

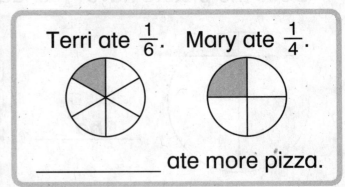

Calli ate $\frac{1}{2}$. Bilal ate $\frac{1}{4}$.

_____ ate more pizza.

Terri ate $\frac{1}{6}$. Mary ate $\frac{1}{4}$.

_____ ate more pizza.

☐ Colour 1 part in each picture.
☐ Write **more** or **less**.

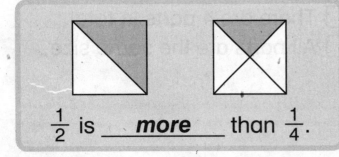

$\frac{1}{2}$ is ___*more*___ than $\frac{1}{4}$.

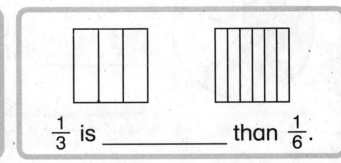

$\frac{1}{3}$ is _____ than $\frac{1}{6}$.

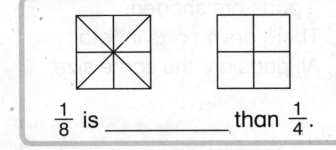

$\frac{1}{8}$ is _____ than $\frac{1}{4}$.

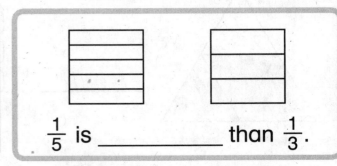

$\frac{1}{5}$ is _____ than $\frac{1}{3}$.

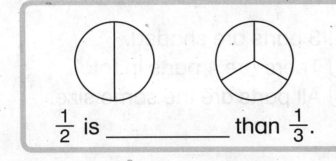

$\frac{1}{2}$ is _____ than $\frac{1}{3}$.

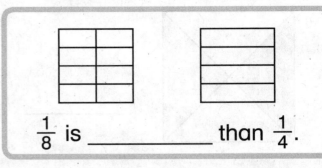

$\frac{1}{8}$ is _____ than $\frac{1}{4}$.

☐ Circle the two questions that compared the same fractions.
  Did you get the same answer? _____

96

○ Fill the measuring cups the correct amount.
○ Circle the cup that is more full.
○ Write **more** or **less**.

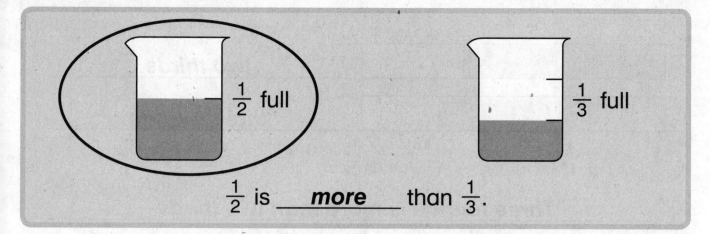

$\frac{1}{2}$ full $\frac{1}{3}$ full

$\frac{1}{2}$ is _____**more**_____ than $\frac{1}{3}$.

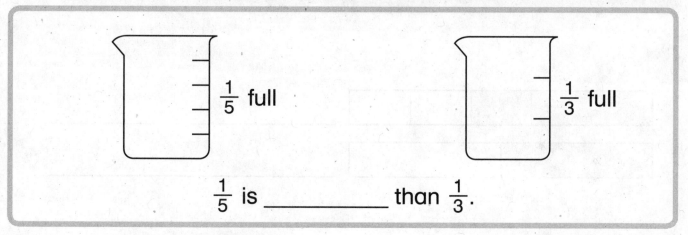

$\frac{1}{5}$ full $\frac{1}{3}$ full

$\frac{1}{5}$ is _____ than $\frac{1}{3}$.

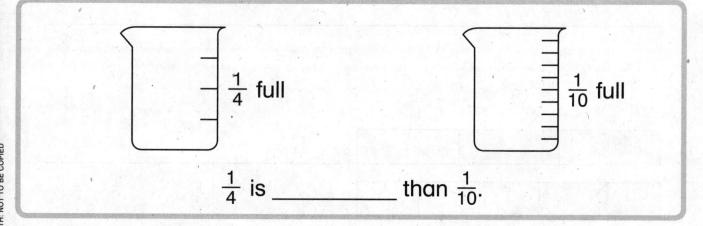

$\frac{1}{4}$ full $\frac{1}{10}$ full

$\frac{1}{4}$ is _____ than $\frac{1}{10}$.

○ Dividing something into more parts makes each part

_____.

     smaller / bigger

What fraction does each picture show?
Which fraction is more?

two thirds

three fourths

Three fourths is more than two thirds .

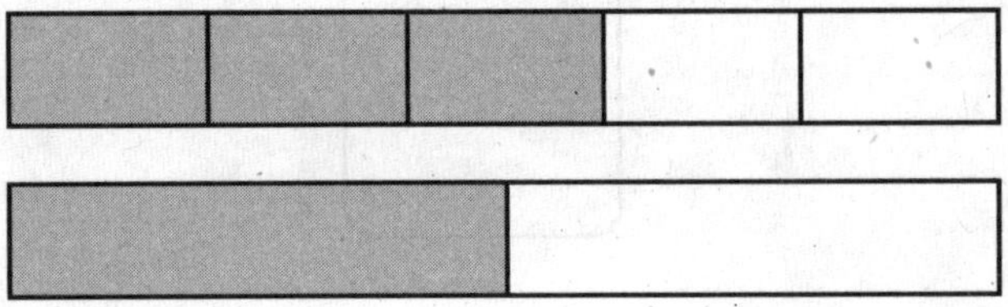

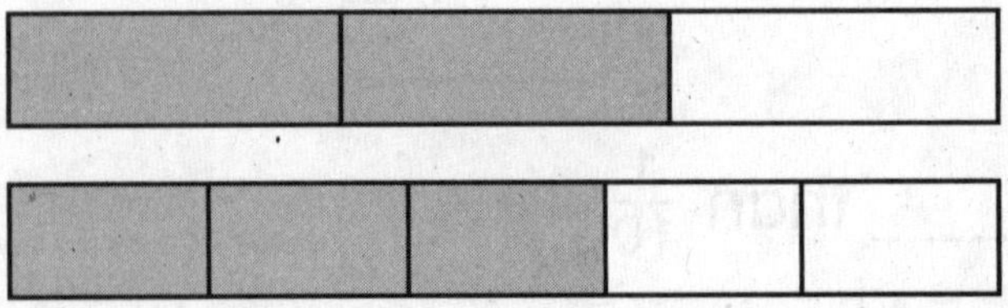

98

Adding Fractions

▢ Move the shaded parts into 1 circle.
▢ Write the missing number.

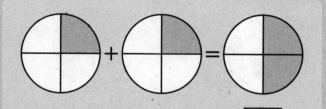

$$\frac{1}{4} + \frac{1}{4} = \frac{\boxed{2}}{4}$$

$$\frac{1}{4} + \frac{2}{4} = \frac{\square}{4}$$

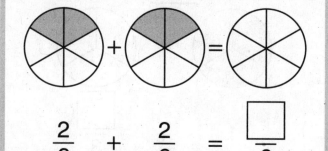

$$\frac{2}{6} + \frac{2}{6} = \frac{\square}{6}$$

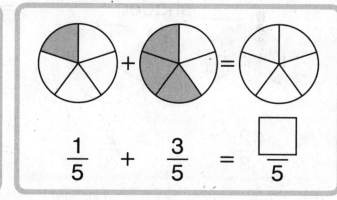

$$\frac{1}{5} + \frac{3}{5} = \frac{\square}{5}$$

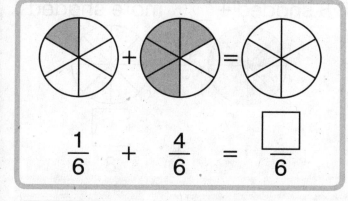

$$\frac{1}{6} + \frac{4}{6} = \frac{\square}{6}$$

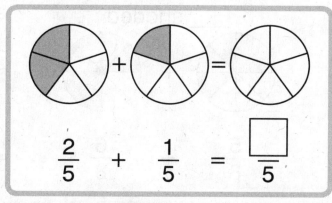

$$\frac{2}{5} + \frac{1}{5} = \frac{\square}{5}$$

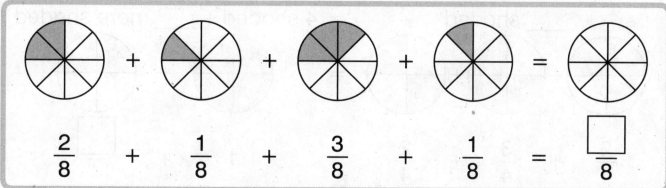

$$\frac{2}{8} + \frac{1}{8} + \frac{3}{8} + \frac{1}{8} = \frac{\square}{8}$$

☐ Find the missing numbers.
☐ Shade the correct number of parts.

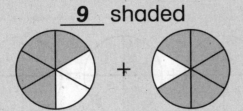

____**9**____ shaded   = 6 shaded + ___**3**___ more shaded

$$\frac{4}{6} + \frac{5}{6} = 1 + \frac{\boxed{3}}{6}$$

____ shaded   = 3 shaded + ____ more shaded

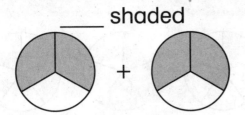

$$\frac{2}{3} + \frac{2}{3} = 1 + \frac{\square}{3}$$

____ shaded   = 8 shaded + ____ more shaded

$$\frac{5}{8} + \frac{6}{8} = 1 + \frac{\square}{8}$$

____ shaded   = 4 shaded + ____ more shaded

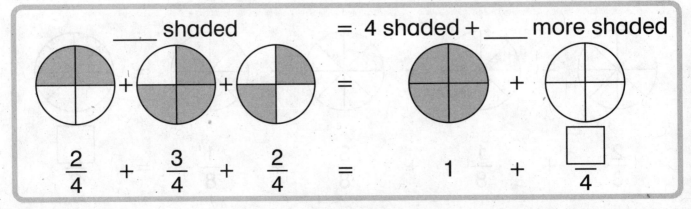

$$\frac{2}{4} + \frac{3}{4} + \frac{2}{4} = 1 + \frac{\square}{4}$$

☐ Find the missing numbers.
☐ Shade the correct number of parts.

_9_ shaded = **_8_ shaded** + **_1_ more shaded**

 =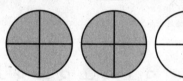

$\dfrac{3}{4}$ + $\dfrac{3}{4}$ + $\dfrac{3}{4}$ = 2 + $\dfrac{\boxed{1}}{4}$

___ shaded = **___ shaded** + **___ more shaded**

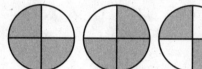 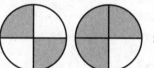 =

$\dfrac{3}{4}$ + $\dfrac{3}{4}$ + $\dfrac{2}{4}$ + $\dfrac{3}{4}$ = 2 + $\dfrac{\boxed{}}{4}$

___ shaded = **___ shaded** + **___ more shaded**

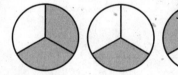 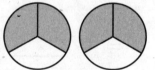 =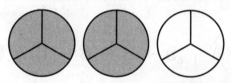

$\dfrac{2}{3}$ + $\dfrac{1}{3}$ + $\dfrac{2}{3}$ + $\dfrac{2}{3}$ = 2 + $\dfrac{\boxed{}}{3}$

___ shaded = **___ shaded** + **___ more shaded**

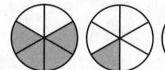 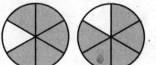 =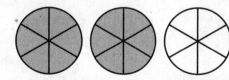

$\dfrac{4}{6}$ + $\dfrac{1}{6}$ + $\dfrac{5}{6}$ + $\dfrac{5}{6}$ = 2 + $\dfrac{\boxed{}}{6}$

Multiplication

$$2 + 2 + 2 + 2 + 2 \quad = \quad 5 \times 2 \quad = \quad 5 \text{ times } 2$$

☐ Fill in the blanks.

$2 + 2 + 2 + 2 = \underline{\quad} \times 2$

$2 + 2 + 2 = \underline{\quad} \times 2$

$2 + 2 + 2 + 2 + 2 + 2 + 2 + 2 + 2 \quad = \quad \underline{\quad} \times 2$

$3 + 3 + 3 + 3 + 3 + 3 \quad = \quad \underline{\quad} \times 3$

$7 + 7 + 7 + 7 + 7 + 7 \quad = \quad \underline{\quad} \times \underline{\quad}$

$8 + 8 + 8 + 8 + 8 + 8 \quad = \quad \underline{\quad} \times \underline{\quad}$

$12 + 12 + 12 + 12 + 12 + 12 + 12 \quad = \quad \underline{\quad} \times \underline{\quad}$

$100 + 100 + 100 \quad = \quad \underline{\quad} \times \underline{\quad}$

$10 + 10 + 10 + 10 + 10 + 10 + 10 + 10 \quad = \quad \underline{\quad} \times \underline{\quad}$

Multiply by counting the dots.

$$
\begin{array}{r}
4 \\
+\,4 \\
\hline
\end{array}
$$

$2 \times 4 = \boxed{}$

rows →   in each row

$$
\begin{array}{r}
6 \\
+\,6 \\
\hline
\end{array}
$$

$2 \times 6 = \boxed{}$

$$
\begin{array}{r}
4 \\
4 \\
+\,4 \\
\hline
\end{array}
$$

$3 \times 4 = \boxed{}$

$$
\begin{array}{r}
3 \\
3 \\
+\,3 \\
\hline
\end{array}
$$

$3 \times 3 = \boxed{}$

$$
\begin{array}{r}
7 \\
+\,7 \\
\hline
\end{array}
$$

$2 \times 7 = \boxed{}$

$$
\begin{array}{r}
3 \\
3 \\
3 \\
+\,3 \\
\hline
\end{array}
$$

$4 \times 3 = \boxed{}$

Now draw the dots, then multiply.

$$
\begin{array}{r}
2 \\
2 \\
+\,2 \\
\hline
\end{array}
$$

$3 \times 2 = \boxed{}$

$$
\begin{array}{r}
5 \\
+\,5 \\
\hline
\end{array}
$$

$2 \times 5 = \boxed{}$

☐ Cover the grid to multiply.

$2 \times 3 = \underline{\hspace{1.5cm}}$

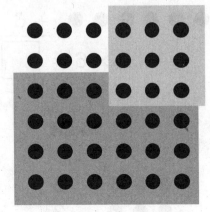

$4 \times 2 = \underline{\hspace{1.5cm}}$

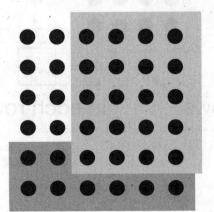

$5 \times 2 = \underline{\hspace{1.5cm}}$

$4 \times 1 = \underline{\hspace{1.5cm}}$

$1 \times 6 = \underline{\hspace{1.5cm}}$

$2 \times 6 = \underline{\hspace{1.5cm}}$

$4 \times 3 = \underline{\hspace{1.5cm}}$

$3 \times 2 = \underline{\hspace{1.5cm}}$

$2 \times 5 = \underline{\hspace{1.5cm}}$

$3 \times 6 = \underline{\hspace{1.5cm}}$

$4 \times 4 = \underline{\hspace{1.5cm}}$

$3 \times 3 = \underline{\hspace{1.5cm}}$

◯ Count the dots.
◯ Write the multiplication in two ways.

7
+ 7

$\boxed{14}$ = 2 + 2 + 2 + 2 + 2 + 2 + 2

__2__ × __7__ = __7__ × __2__

3
+ 3

$\square$ = 2 + 2 + 2

____ × ____ = ____ × ____

4
4
+ 4

$\square$ = 3 + 3 + 3 + 3

____ × ____ = ____ × ____

6
+ 6

$\square$ = 2 + 2 + 2 + 2 + 2 + 2

____ × ____ = ____ × ____

5
5
+ 5

$\square$ = 3 + 3 + 3 + 3 + 3

____ × ____ = ____ × ____

4
+ 4

$\square$ = 2 + 2 + 2 + 2

____ × ____ = ____ × ____

◯ Circle the number sentences that make sense.

5 + 3 = 3 + 5

5 − 3 = 3 − 5

5 × 3 = 3 × 5

◻ What is wrong with the other sentence?

Multiplication by Skip Counting

☐ Keep track as you go along.

| 6 | 9 | 12 | 15 |

$5 \times 3 =$ __3__ + __3__ + __3__ + __3__ + __3__ = **15**

☐ ☐ ☐

$4 \times 5 =$ ___ + ___ + ___ + ___ = ☐

☐ ☐ ☐ ☐ ☐

$6 \times 10 =$ ___ + ___ + ___ + ___ + ___ + ___ = ☐

☐ ☐ ☐ ☐ ☐

$6 \times 2 =$ ___ + ___ + ___ + ___ + ___ + ___ = ☐

☐ ☐ ☐ ☐

$5 \times 4 =$ ___ + ___ + ___ + ___ + ___ = ☐

☐ ☐ ☐

$4 \times 3 =$ ___ + ___ + ___ + ___ = ☐

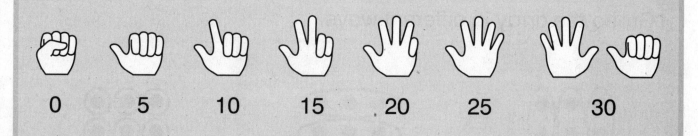

0   5   10   15   20   25   30

☐ Multiply.

$3 \times 5 =$ _____

$4 \times 5 =$ _____

$5 \times 5 =$ _____

$1 \times 5 =$ _____

$0 \times 5 =$ _____

$6 \times 5 =$ _____

☐ Count by 3s.

_0_   _3_   ___   ___   ___   ___   ___

☐ Multiply.

$2 \times 3 =$ _____

$4 \times 3 =$ _____

$1 \times 3 =$ _____

$6 \times 3 =$ _____

$3 \times 3 =$ _____

$0 \times 3 =$ _____

Multiplication — Advanced

☐ Group the array in different ways.

___3___ × ___2___ = 6

_____ × _____ = 6

_____ × _____ = 6

_____ × _____ = 12

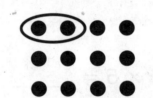

_____ × _____ = 12

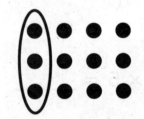

_____ × _____ = 12

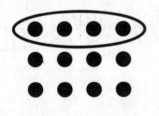

_____ × _____ = 12

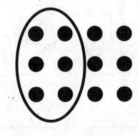

_____ × _____ = 12

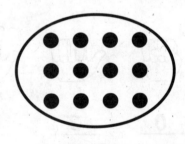

_____ × _____ = 12

_____

_____

_____

☐ Explain each way of counting.

$\begin{array}{r} 4 \\ \times\ 4 \\ \hline \end{array}$

There are 4 groups of 4.

Each group has 4 dots.

☐ $= 2 \times 5$

$+$ ☐ $= 2 \times 3$

————

☐

☐ $= 5 \times 5$

$-$ ☐ $= 3 \times 3$

————

☐

Does each way get the same answer? _____

Draw leaps on the number line to find the answer.

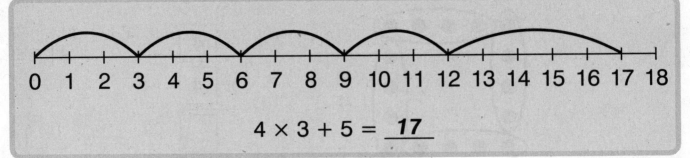

$4 \times 3 + 5 =$ __17__

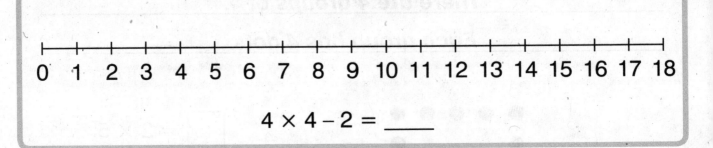

$4 \times 4 - 2 =$ _____

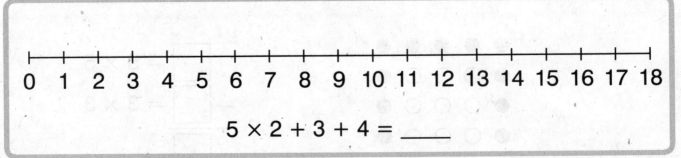

$7 \times 2 + 3 =$ _____

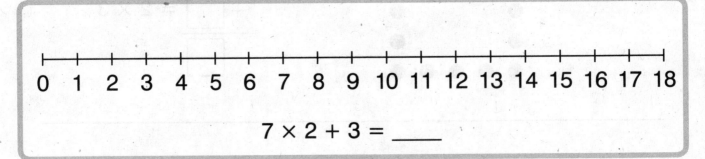

$5 \times 2 + 3 + 4 =$ _____

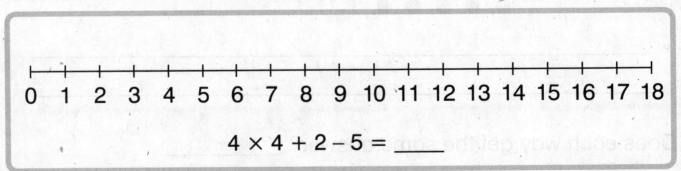

$4 \times 4 + 2 - 5 =$ _____

Division

3 friends want to share 6 apples equally.

Each friend takes 1 apple.

Each friend can take another apple.

Each friend gets 2 apples.

☐ Put 1 apple in each basket until they are gone.
☐ Draw circles for apples.

How many does each person get?

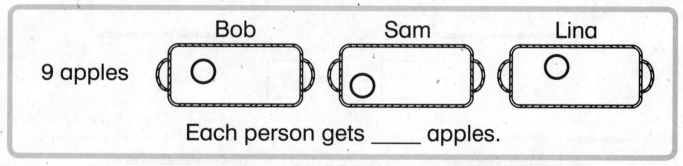

9 apples

Bob   Sam   Lina

Each person gets _____ apples.

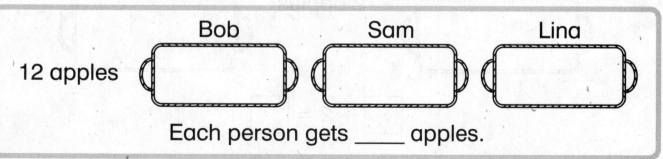

12 apples

Bob   Sam   Lina

Each person gets _____ apples.

2 friends want to share apples.

☐ Put the same number of apples in each basket.
☐ Finish the division sentence.

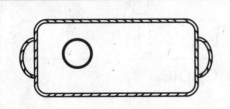 6 apples

number of apples → $\boxed{6}$ ÷ 2 = ☐ ← number in each basket

 10 apples

☐ ÷ 2 = ☐

 8 apples

☐ ÷ 2 = ☐

 12 apples

☐ ÷ 2 = ☐

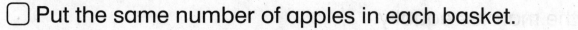

☐ Put the same number of apples in each basket.
☐ Write the division sentence.

12 apples

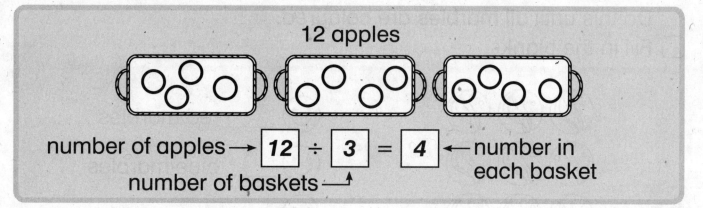

number of apples ⟶ $\boxed{12} \div \boxed{3} = \boxed{4}$ ⟵ number in each basket

number of baskets ⟶

8 apples

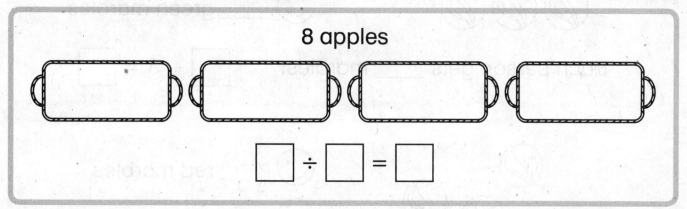

$\boxed{} \div \boxed{} = \boxed{}$

9 apples

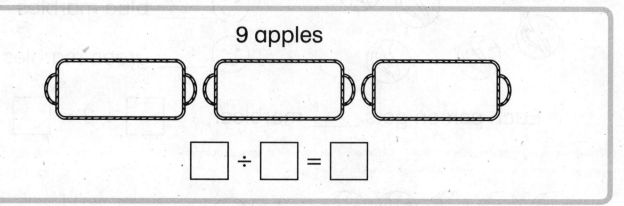

$\boxed{} \div \boxed{} = \boxed{}$

12 apples

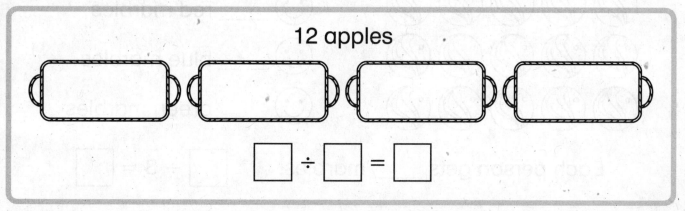

$\boxed{} \div \boxed{} = \boxed{}$

☐ Divide the marbles equally.

☐ Colour 1 marble red, 1 marble blue, and 1 marble green.
   Do this until all marbles are coloured.

☐ Fill in the blanks.

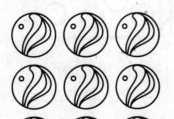 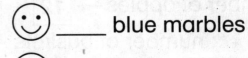

_____ red marbles

_____ blue marbles

_____ green marbles

Each person gets _____ marbles.   ☐ ÷ 3 = ☐

 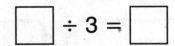

_____ red marbles

_____ blue marbles

_____ green marbles

Each person gets _____ marbles.   ☐ ÷ 3 = ☐

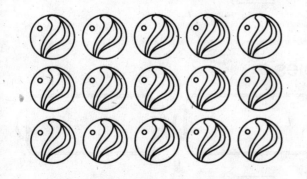

_____ red marbles

_____ blue marbles

_____ green marbles

Each person gets _____ marbles.   ☐ ÷ 3 = ☐

114

How Many Groups?

☐ Divide the people into groups of 3.

How many groups? _____

How many groups? _____

How many groups? _____

How many groups? _____

How many groups? _____

☐ Find how many groups.

How many groups of 2? __4__

How many groups of 5? ____

How many groups of 4? ____

How many groups of 2? ____

How many groups of 4? ____

How many groups of 2? ____

116

Problems and Puzzles

Gita picked 34 strawberries.
Mayah picked double that.
How many did Mayah pick?

Ron is twelve years old.
Katie is 5 years younger.
How old is Katie?

Mita ate $\frac{3}{8}$ of a pizza.
Nomi ate the rest.
How much did Nomi eat?

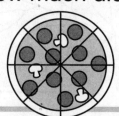

Two people share eight pears.
How many pears
does each person get?

Base ten blocks cost 5¢ each.
How much will it cost to make a
model for the number 31?

A teddy bear costs 25¢.
Ahmed pays for it with 3 dimes.
How much change does he get back?

Apples are cut into 4 pieces. Six people share three apples.
How many pieces does each person get?

Growing Patterns

How many...

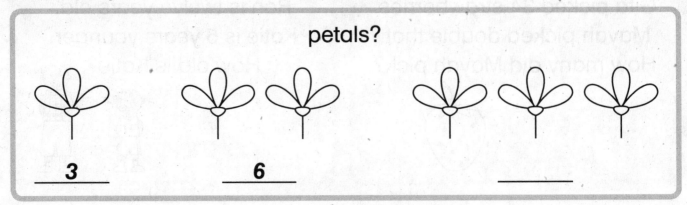

petals?

_3_   _6_   _____

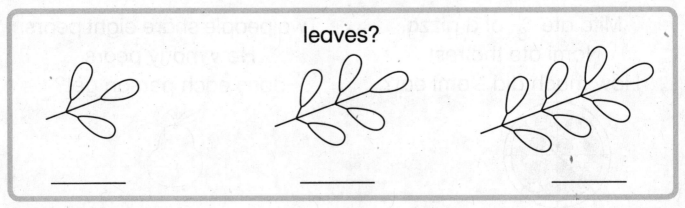

leaves?

_____   _____   _____

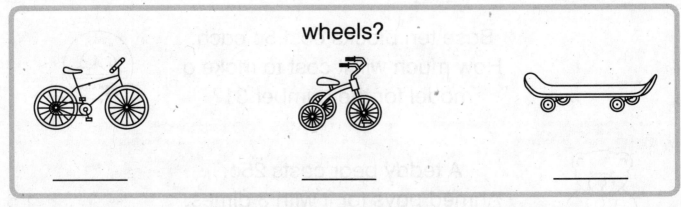

wheels?

_____   _____   _____

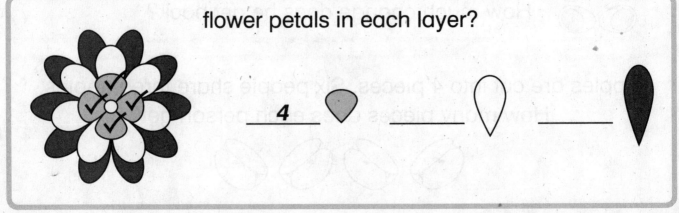

flower petals in each layer?

_4_ 🔶 _____ ⬜ _____ ⬛

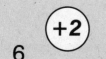 6   8      6 + 2 = 8

                    6   7   8   8 is 2 more than 6.

☐ Write the number you add in the circles.

8 (+1) 9	6 (+) 9	7 (+) 9	3 (+) 7
2 (+) 4	11 ( ) 13	10 ( ) 16	5 ( ) 8
4 ( ) 7	12 ( ) 18	10 ( ) 17	10 ( ) 20

2 ( ) 4 ( ) 6   5 ( ) 10 ( ) 15

15 ( ) 16 ( ) 17   8 ( ) 10 ( ) 12

8 ( ) 10 ( ) 12

 says the next number is 14. How does she know?

_____

makes patterns by adding the **same** number.

☐ Continue the pattern.

| 2 | (+1) | 3 | (+1) | _4_ |

| 3 | (+2) | 5 | (+2) | ___ |

| 7 | (+1) | 8 | ◯ | ___ |

| 2 | (+2) | 4 | ◯ | ___ |

| 3 | (+10) | 13 | ◯ | ___ |

| 0 | (+3) | 3 | ◯ | ___ |

☐ Find the number adds and continue the pattern.

| 5 | ◯ | 10 | ◯ | ___ |

| 1 | ◯ | 3 | ◯ | ___ |

| 4 | ◯ | 14 | ◯ | ___ | ◯ | ___ | ◯ | ___ | ◯ | ___ |

| 7 | ◯ | 9 | ◯ | ___ | ◯ | ___ | ◯ | ___ | ◯ | ___ |

| 20 | ◯ | 25 | ◯ | ___ | ◯ | ___ | ◯ | ___ | ◯ | ___ |

Patterns and Algebra 2-9

Shrinking Patterns

How many...

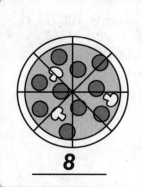  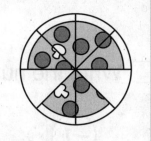

pieces of pizza?

8   **7**   _____

apples on a plate?

_____   _____   _____

dots in a row?

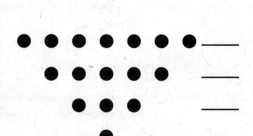 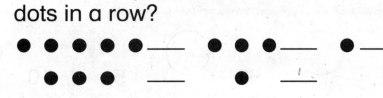

children in the line?

  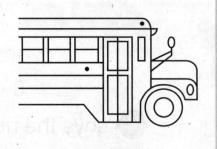

_____   _____   _____

Patterns and Algebra 2-10

121

8 $\boxed{-3}$ 5	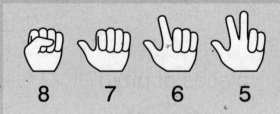 $\quad 8 \quad 7 \quad 6 \quad 5$	$8 - 3 = 5$ 5 is 3 less than 8.

☐ Write the number you subtract in the circles.

$6 \quad \boxed{-1} \quad 5$

$4 \quad \bigcirc{-} \quad 3$

$5 \quad \bigcirc{-} \quad 2$

$6 \quad \bigcirc{-} \quad 4$

$7 \quad \bigcirc{-} \quad 6$

$8 \quad \bigcirc{-} \quad 4$

$12 \quad \bigcirc{-} \quad 10$

$12 \quad \bigcirc{-} \quad 11$

$16 \quad \bigcirc \quad 14$

$19 \quad \bigcirc \quad 15$

$18 \quad \bigcirc \quad 12$

$17 \quad \bigcirc \quad 10$

$7 \quad \bigcirc \quad 6 \quad \bigcirc \quad 5$

$10 \quad \bigcirc \quad 9 \quad \bigcirc \quad 8$

$6 \quad \bigcirc \quad 4 \quad \bigcirc \quad 2$

$13 \quad \bigcirc \quad 12 \quad \bigcirc \quad 11$

$8 \quad \bigcirc \quad 6 \quad \bigcirc \quad 4$

 says the next number is 2. How does he know?

_____

Describing Patterns

☐ Write the number you add in the circles.
☐ Describe the pattern.

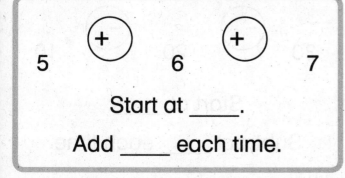

1   **+2**   3   **+2**   5

Start at __1__.

Add __2__ each time.

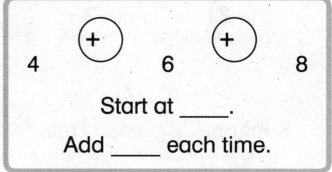

4   **+**   6   **+**   8

Start at ____.

Add ____ each time.

5   **+**   6   **+**   7

Start at ____.

Add ____ each time.

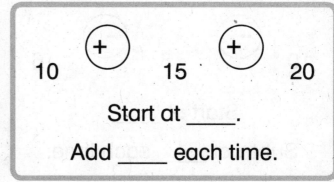

10   **+**   15   **+**   20

Start at ____.

Add ____ each time.

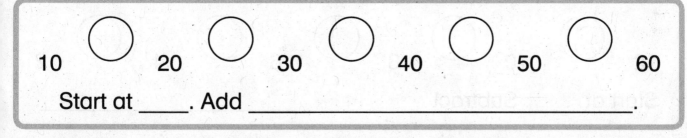

10 ⃝ 20 ⃝ 30 ⃝ 40 ⃝ 50 ⃝ 60

Start at ____. Add _____.

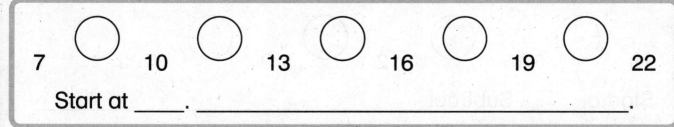

7 ⃝ 10 ⃝ 13 ⃝ 16 ⃝ 19 ⃝ 22

Start at ____. _____

0 ⃝ 5 ⃝ 10 ⃝ 15 ⃝ 20 ⃝ 25

_____. _____.

☐ Write the number you subtract in the circles.
☐ Describe the pattern.

(−2)   (−2)
7   5   3

Start at __7__.
Subtract __2__ each time.

(−)   (−)
8   7   6

Start at ____.
Subtract ____ each time.

(−)   (−)
10   8   6

Start at ____.
Subtract ____ each time.

(−)   (−)
30   20   10

Start at ____.
Subtract ____ each time.

( ) ( ) ( ) ( ) ( )
12   10   8   6   4   2

Start at ____. Subtract _____.

( ) ( ) ( ) ( ) ( )
18   15   12   9   6   3

Start at ____. Subtract _____.

( ) ( ) ( ) ( ) ( )
35   30   25   20   15   10

Start at ____. _____.

□ Write the number you add or subtract in the circles.

□ Describe the pattern.

7 (−1) 6 (−1) 5

Start at __7__.

Subtract __1__ each time.

7 (−) 5 (−) 3

Start at ____.

Subtract ____ each time.

15 (+) 16 (+) 17 (+) 18 (+) 19

Start at ____. Add ____ each time.

1 (+) 3 (+) 5 (+) 7 (+) 9

Start at ____. Add ____ each time.

8 (−) 7 (−) 6 (−) 5 (−) 4

Start at ____. Subtract _____.

8 (+) 9 (+) 10 (+) 11 (+) 12

Start at ____. Add _____.

8 (−) 6 (−) 4 (−) 2 (−) 0

Start at ____. Subtract _____.

☐ Continue the pattern.

Start at 1. Add 2 each time.

1 ⟨+2⟩ 3 ⟨+2⟩ 5 ⟨+2⟩ 7 ⟨+2⟩ 9

Start at 5. Add 1 each time.

5 ⟨+1⟩ 6 ⟨+1⟩ ___ ⟨+1⟩ ___ ⟨+1⟩ ___

Start at 10. Subtract 2 each time.

10 ⟨−2⟩ ___ ⟨−2⟩ ___ ⟨ ⟩ ___ ⟨ ⟩ ___

Start at 3. Add 10 each time.

⟨ ⟩ ___ ⟨ ⟩ ___ ⟨ ⟩ ___ ⟨ ⟩ ___

Start at 16. Subtract 2 each time.

⟨ ⟩ ___ ⟨ ⟩ ___ ⟨ ⟩ ___ ⟨ ⟩ ___

☐ Make your own rule and continue the pattern.

Start at ____. Add ____ each time.

⟨ ⟩ ___ ⟨ ⟩ ___ ⟨ ⟩ ___ ⟨ ⟩ ___

Identifying Patterns

☐ Write…

    R if the pattern **R**epeats.

    G if the pattern **G**rows.

    S if the pattern **S**hrinks.

| 4 | 5 | 6 | 7 | 8 | 9 | 10 | 11 | **G** |

| 4 | 3 | 2 | 4 | 3 | 2 | 4 | 3 | 2 | ___ |

| 10 | 9 | 8 | 7 | 6 | 5 | 4 | 3 | 2 | ___ |

| 3 | 5 | 7 | 9 | 11 | 13 | 15 | 17 | ___ |

| 3 | 5 | 7 | 3 | 5 | 7 | 3 | 5 | 7 | 3 | 5 | 7 | ___ |

| 100 | 90 | 80 | 70 | 60 | 50 | 40 | ___ |

| 5 | 10 | 15 | 20 | 25 | 30 | 35 | ___ |

☐ Add or subtract.
☐ Does each pattern repeat, grow, or shrink?
Write **R**, **G**, or **S** beside each pattern.

3	3	3	3	3	3	3	**R**
+1	+2	+3	+4	+5	+6	+7	**G**
4	5	6	7	8	9	10	**G**

9	8	7	6	5	4	3	___
+2	+2	+2	+2	+2	+2	+2	___
							___

9	8	7	6	5	4	3	2	___
+1	+2	+3	+4	+5	+6	+7	+8	___
								___

3	5	7	9	11	13	15	___
-2	-2	-2	-2	-2	-2	-2	___
							___

12	11	10	9	8	7	6	___
-0	-1	-2	-3	-4	-5	-6	___
							___

Patterns and Algebra 2-12

☐ Describe the pattern.

1　　3　　5　　7　　9

Start at __1__.

Add __2__ each time.

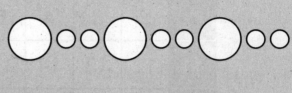

_____ *big, little, little*

_____ *then repeat*

8　　7　　6　　5　　4

Start at ____.

Subtract _____.

30　　40　　50　　60　　70

Start at ____.

Add _____.

12　　10　　8　　6　　4

_____

_____

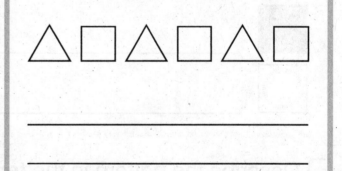

_____

_____

5　　10　　15　　20　　25

_____

_____

100　　　98　　　96　　　94

_____

_____

Patterns in a Hundreds Chart

1	2	3	4	5	6	7	8	9	10
11	(12)	13	14	15	16	17	18	19	20
21	22	(23)	24	25	26	27	28	29	30
31	32	33	(34)	35	36	37	38	39	40
41	42	43	44	(45)	46	47	48	49	50
51	52	53	54	55	(56)	57	58	59	60

☐ Describe the pattern in the **ones digits**.

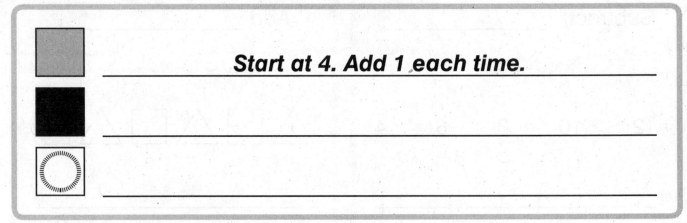

Start at 4. Add 1 each time.

☐ Describe the pattern in the **tens digits**.

1	2	3	4	5	6	7	8	9	10
11	(12)	13	14	15	16	17	18	19	20
21	22	(23)	24	25	26	27	28	29	30
31	32	33	(34)	35	36	37	38	39	40
41	42	43	44	(45)	46	47	48	49	50
51	52	53	54	55	(56)	57	58	59	60

☐ Circle the correct word.
☐ Copy the pattern.
☐ Write the numbers you add in the circles.
☐ Describe the pattern.

�® are all in the same column / diagonal / **(row.)**

__24__ , (+1) __25__ , (+1) __26__ , (+1) __27__ , (+1) __28__ , (+1) __29__

Start at 24. Add 1 each time.

■ are all in the same column / diagonal / row.

__1__ , ◯ __11__ , ◯ ____ , ◯ ____ , ◯ ____ , ◯ ____

Start at _____ .

▣ are all in the same column / diagonal / row.

____ , ◯ ____ , ◯ ____ , ◯ ____ , ◯ ____

_____

Patterns and Algebra 2-13

Finding Mistakes

☐ Write the number you add or subtract in the circles.
☐ Write the missing number.

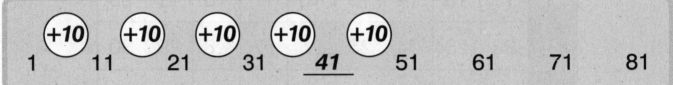

(+10) (+10) (+10) (+10) (+10)

1   11   21   31   _41_   51   61   71   81

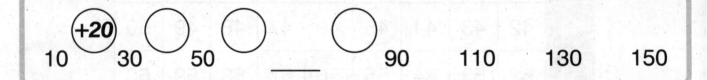

(+20) ◯ ◯   ◯

10   30   50   ___   90   110   130   150

◯ ◯ ◯   ◯

10   9   8   ___   6   5   4   3   2   1

◯ ◯ ◯   ◯   ◯

20   18   16   14   ___   10   8   6   4   2

☐ Now draw the circles and write the numbers.

0   25   50   ___   100   125   150   175

200   175   150   125   ___   75   50

Bonus

1   4   7   ___   13   16   19   22   25

What is the missing room number?

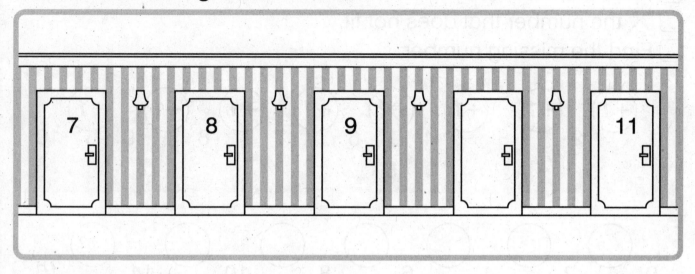

What is the missing house number?

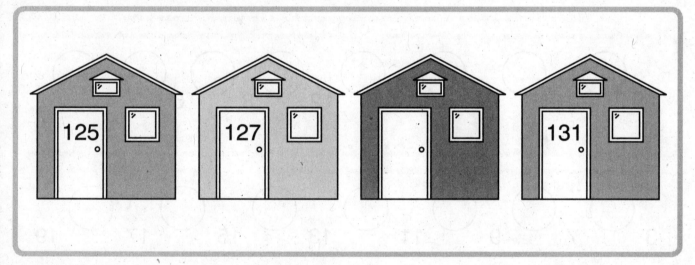

☐ Find the missing book pages.

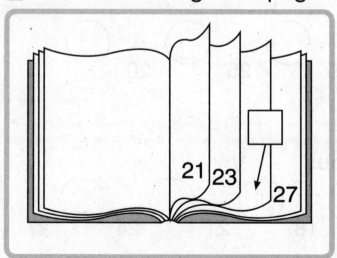
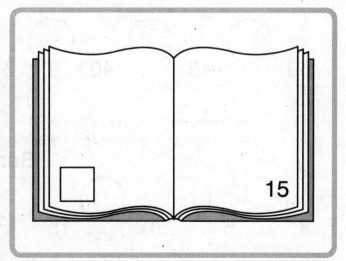

Write the numbers you add or subtract in the circles.

X the number that does not fit.

Find the missing number.

1 (+1) 2 (+1) 3 (+1) 4 (+2̶) 6 (+1) 7 (+1) 8 (+1) 9 (+1) 10

↑
5

0 ◯ 2 ◯ 4 ◯ 6 ◯ 8 ◯ 10 ◯ 14 ◯ 16

20 ◯ 18 ◯ 16 ◯ 14 ◯ 12 ◯ 8 ◯ 6 ◯ 4 ◯ 2

3 ◯ 7 ◯ 9 ◯ 11 ◯ 13 ◯ 15 ◯ 17 ◯ 19

50 ◯ 45 ◯ 40 ◯ 35 ◯ 25 ◯ 20 ◯ 15

Bonus

3 ◯ 6 ◯ 12 ◯ 15 ◯ 18 ◯ 21 ◯ 24 ◯ 27

134

☐ Write the numbers you add or subtract in the circles.
☐ ✗ the mistakes in the pattern.
☐ Correct the mistakes.

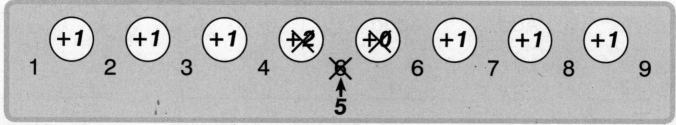

1 (+1) 2 (+1) 3 (+1) 4 (⊗2) ⊗5 (⊗0) 6 (+1) 7 (+1) 8 (+1) 9

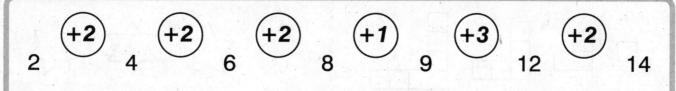

2 (+2) 4 (+2) 6 (+2) 8 (+1) 9 (+3) 12 (+2) 14

5 ◯ 10 ◯ 15 ◯ 22 ◯ 25 ◯ 30

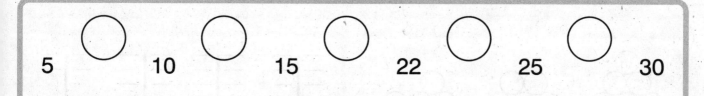

2 ◯ 7 ◯ 12 ◯ 17 ◯ 22 ◯ 28 ◯ 32

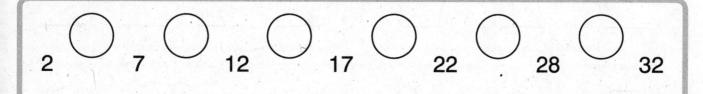

25 ◯ 50 ◯ 70 ◯ 100 ◯ 125 ◯ 150

Bonus

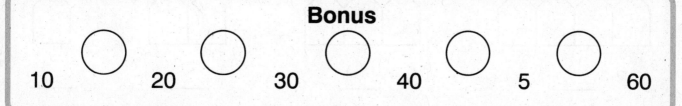

10 ◯ 20 ◯ 30 ◯ 40 ◯ 5 ◯ 60

Showing Patterns in Different Ways

☐ Write numbers to show the pattern.

Aa	Aaa	Aaaa
_2_	_3_	_4_

____ ____ ____

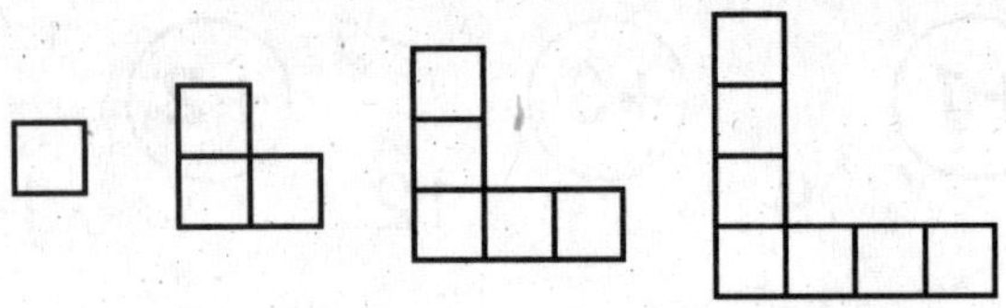

____ ____ ____ ____

____ ____ ____ ____

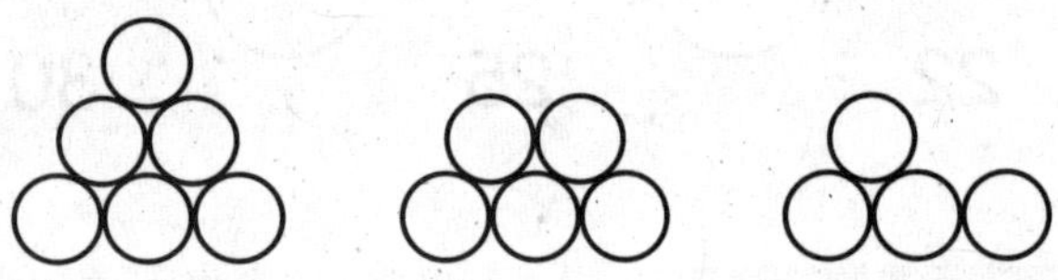

____ ____ ____

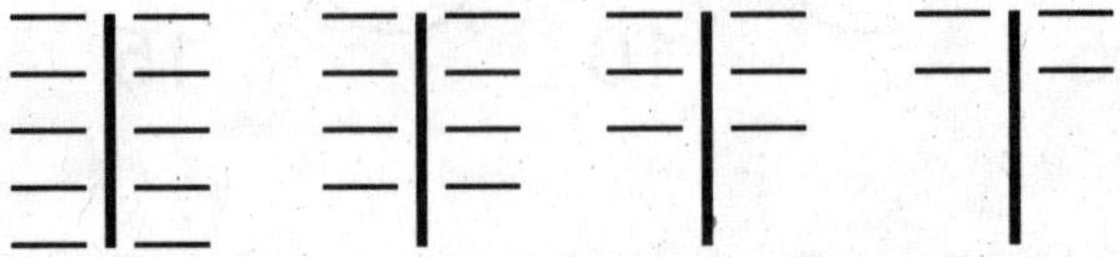

____ ____ ____ ____

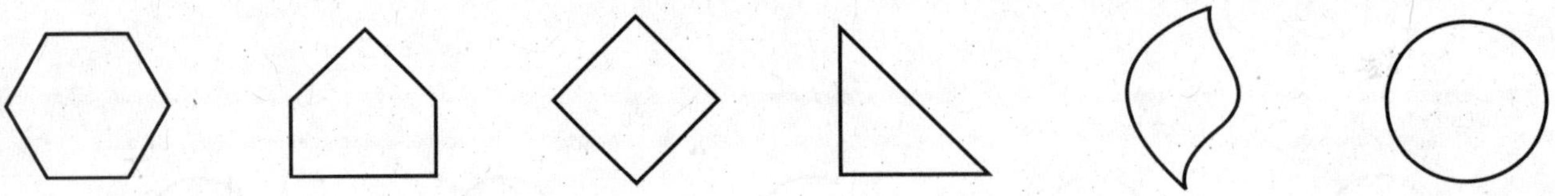

____ ____ ____ ____ ____ ____

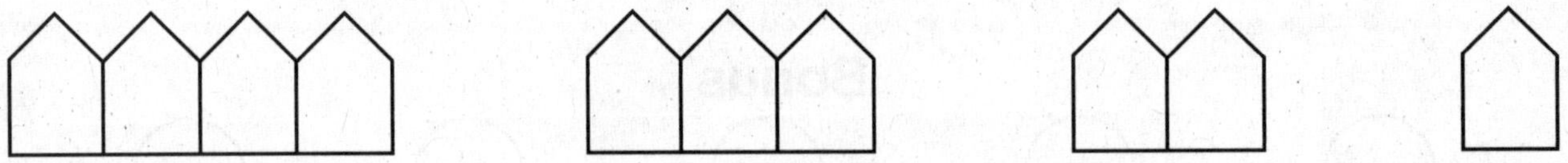

____ ____ ____

Comparing Lines

The lines show the time Helen and Ru were singing.

☐ Circle Helen's line.

Helen and Ru start singing.

Helen stops first.

Helen starts singing first.

Ru stops before Helen.

Ru starts singing first.

They stop at the same time.

Helen starts singing first.

They stop at the same time.

Ru starts singing first.

Helen stops before Ru.

Measuring Time

☐ Sing the alphabet.
☐ Write the letter you get to when your partner...

does 5 jumping jacks  **J**	spins around 3 times  _____
traces these shapes 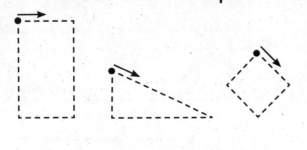 _____	stands up and sits down  _____
writes "hello" backward  _____	writes their name backward _____

What took the **longest** time? _____

What took the **shortest** time? _____

Estimating Time

How many in one sand-timer ?

	Estimate	Measure
jumping jacks		
squats		
words with **b**		
jumps		

Your Own Unit

☐ Draw or describe your measuring unit.

☐ Measure using your own unit.

stand up and sit down

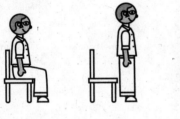

_____ units

write the alphabet

_____ units

sing "O Canada"

_____ units

read a story

_____ units

📓 Is your measuring unit better for measuring tasks that take a long time or a short time? Explain.

Clock Faces

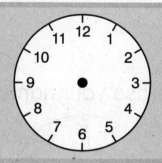

This is a clock face.

Numbers start at 1 and end at 12.

☐ Fill in the missing 3, 6, 9, and 12.

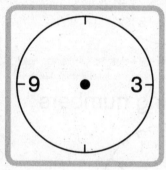 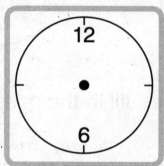 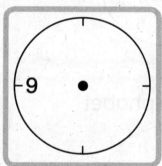 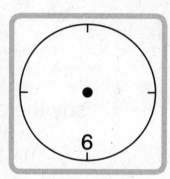

☐ Fill in the missing numbers. Start with 3, 6, 9, and 12.

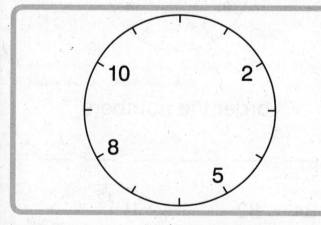 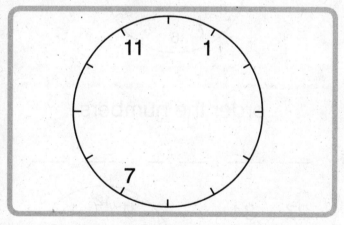

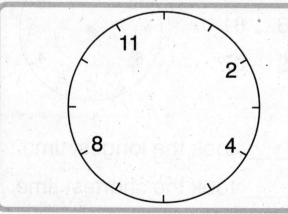 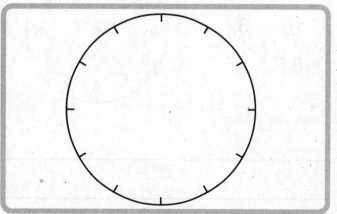

Measuring Time with Clocks

Start when the fast hand is at 12.

☐ Draw the fast hand when you finish.

write your name: _____ 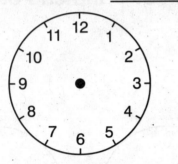	erase your name 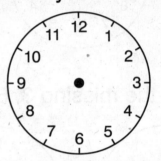
say the alphabet 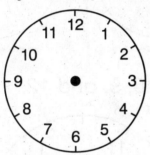	fill in the missing numbers 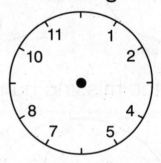

order the numbers

_____ ___ ___ ___ ___ ___

27   34

16   52

81   45

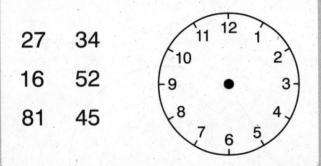

order the numbers

_____ ___ ___ ___ ___ ___

84   82

86   81

89   87

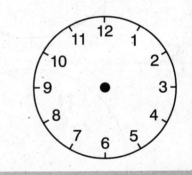

_____ took the longest time.

_____ took the shortest time.

Jacob starts juggling.
Then he drops the balls.
How long does Jacob juggle?

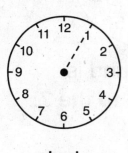

starts

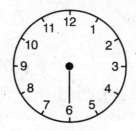

stops

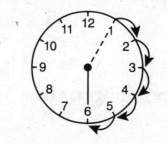

Jacob juggles for _____

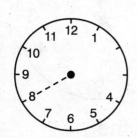

starts

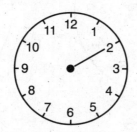

stops

Jacob juggles for _____

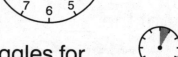

☐ Did Jacob get better on his second try? Explain your answer.

_____

_____

_____

The Hour Hand

The **hour hand** is short and thick.

hour hand

The hour hand is pointing **at the 3**.

The hour hand is pointing **close to the 7**.

Where is the hour hand pointing?

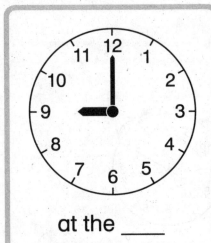

at the _____

close to the _____

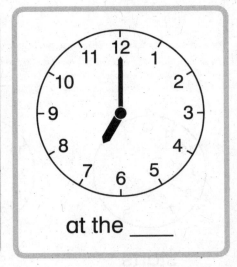

at the _____

close to the _____

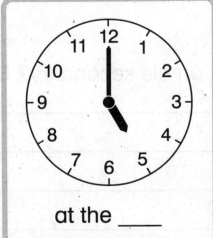

at the _____

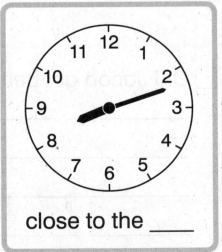

close to the _____

Write **before** or **after**.

 It is a little _____***before***_____ 7 o'clock.

 It is a little _____ 1 o'clock.

 It is a little _____ 4 o'clock.

 It is a little _____ 12 o'clock.

 It is a little _____ 6 o'clock.

 It is a little _____ 11 o'clock.

What time is it?

__10__ o'clock

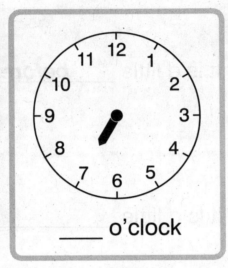

____ o'clock

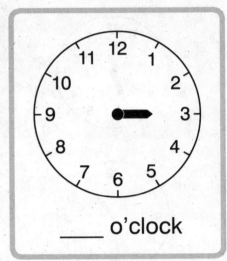

____ o'clock

a little **after**
____ o'clock

a little **before**
____ o'clock

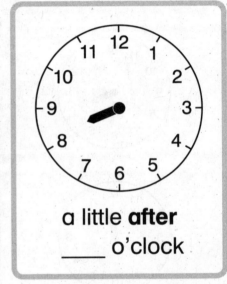

a little **after**
____ o'clock

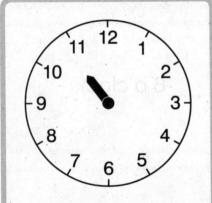

a little **before**
____ o'clock

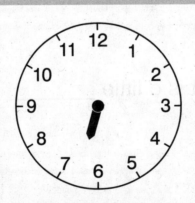

half way between
____ o'clock and
____ o'clock

half way between
____ o'clock and
____ o'clock

☐ Write the time.

_____
a little

_____
after 2   o'clock

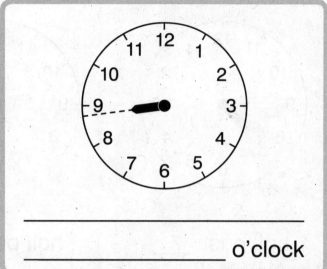

_____
_____ o'clock

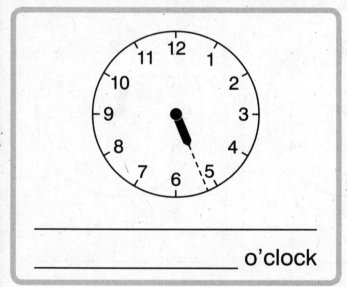

_____
_____ o'clock

_____
_____ o'clock

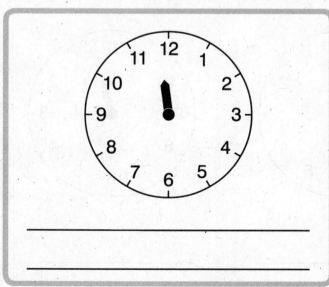

_____
_____

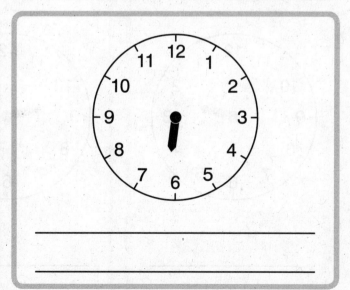

_____
_____

Write the time.

half past __7__

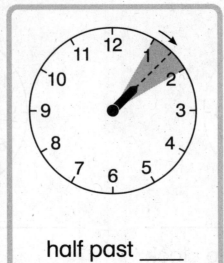

half past ____

half past ____

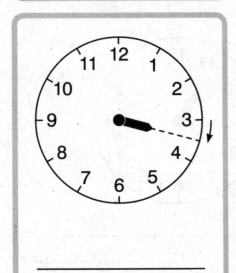

_____

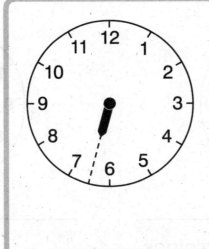

_____

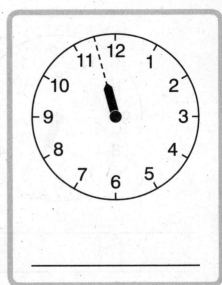

_____

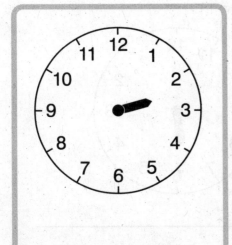

_____

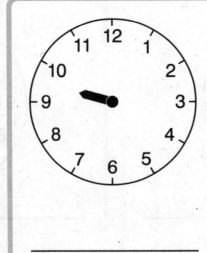

_____

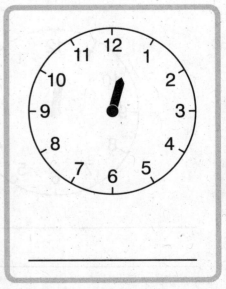

_____

Time to the Hour

It is **9 o'clock** or **9:00**.

☐ Write the time in two ways.

__6__ o'clock
__6__ : 00

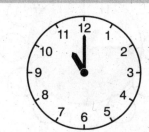

_____ o'clock
_____ : 00

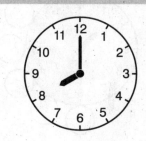

_____ o'clock
_____ : 00

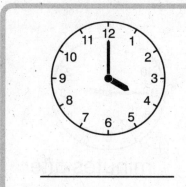

_____
_____ : _____

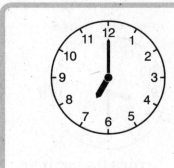

_____
_____ : _____

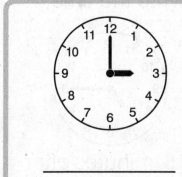

_____
_____ : _____

☐ Use a toy clock to show these times.
☐ Circle the two that are the same.

7:00	3 o'clock	5:00
1:00	6 o'clock	1 o'clock

The Minute Hand

How many minutes after 10:00?

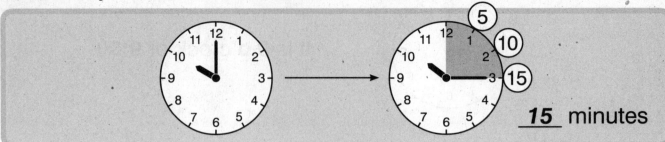

_**15**_ minutes

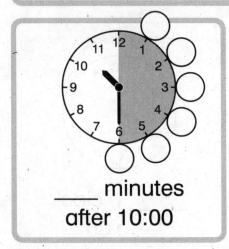

____ minutes
after 10:00

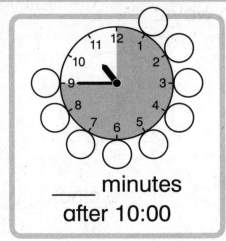

____ minutes
after 10:00

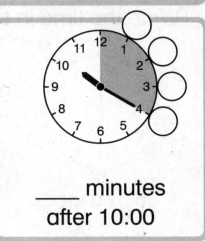

____ minutes
after 10:00

☐ Write the time.

_**15**_ minutes after
_**7:00**_ is _**7**_ : _**15**_

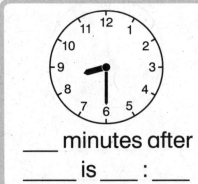

____ minutes after
_____ is ____ : ____

____ minutes after
_____ is ____ : ____

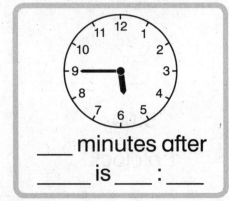

____ minutes after
_____ is ____ : ____

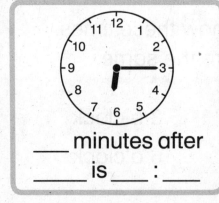

____ minutes after
_____ is ____ : ____

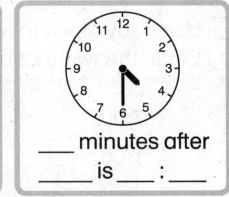

____ minutes after
_____ is ____ : ____

Time to the Half Hour

It is half an hour after 8:00 or 30 minutes after 8:00.

half past 8

8:30

☐ Write the time in two ways.

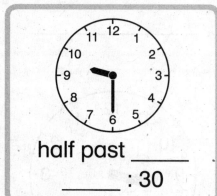

half past _____

_____ : 30

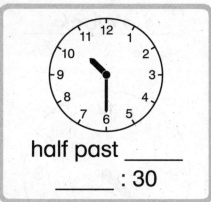

half past _____

_____ : 30

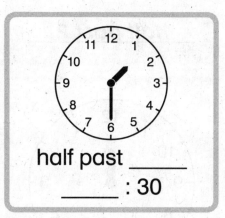

half past _____

_____ : 30

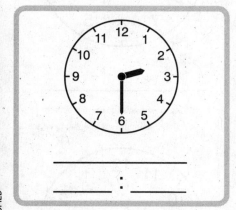

_____ : _____

_____ : _____

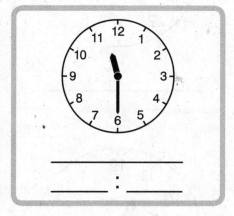

_____ : _____

☐ Use a toy clock to show these times.
☐ Circle the two that are the same.

12:30	half past 2	4:30
5:30	half past 9	half past 12

Look at where the hour hand is.

◯ Draw the minute hand at 12 or 6.
◯ Write the time.

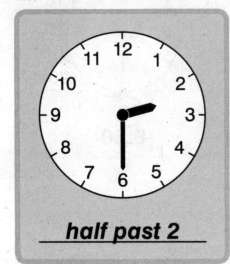

___half past 2___

___4 o'clock___

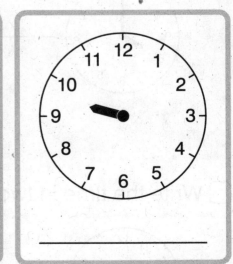

_____

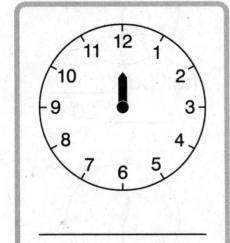

_____

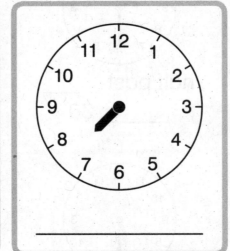

_____

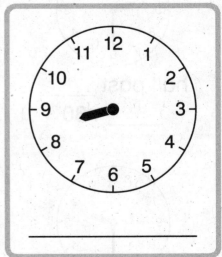

_____

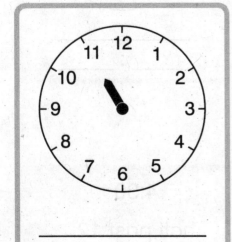

_____

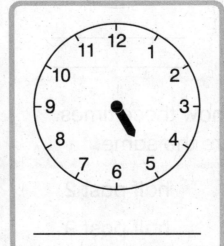

_____

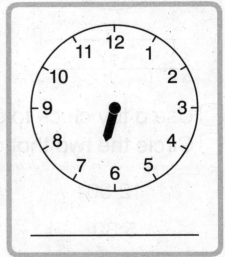

_____

Quarter Past

It is a quarter of an hour after 7:00 or 15 minutes after 7:00.

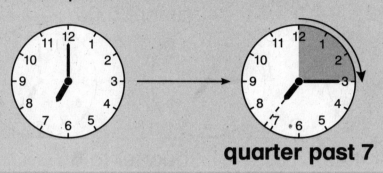

quarter past 7

7:15

☐ Write the time in two ways.

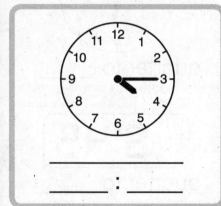

quarter past __1__

__1__ : __15__

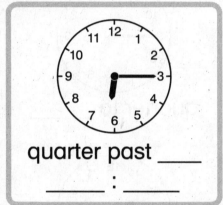

quarter past ____

____ : ____

quarter past ____

____ : ____

____ : ____

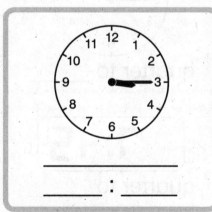

____ : ____

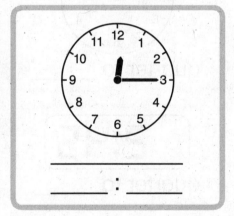

____ : ____

☐ Use a toy clock to show the times.
☐ Circle the two that are the same.

11:15	quarter past 7	quarter past 2
quarter past 9	8:15	7:15

Quarter To

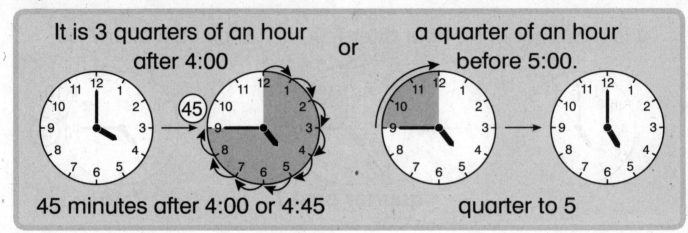

It is 3 quarters of an hour after 4:00 **or** a quarter of an hour before 5:00.

45 minutes after 4:00 or 4:45   quarter to 5

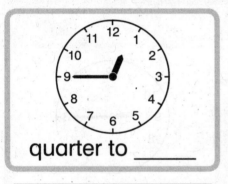

quarter to _____

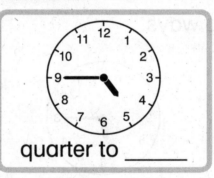

quarter to _____

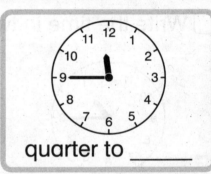

quarter to _____

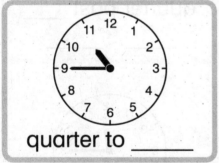

quarter to _____

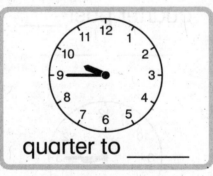

quarter to _____

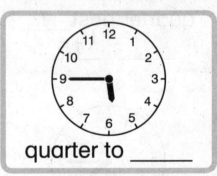

quarter to _____

2:45

quarter to _____

7:45

quarter to _____

8:45

quarter to _____

3:45

quarter to _____

9:45

quarter to _____

6:45

quarter to _____

☐ Circle the times that are the same.

A **quarter** of an hour **before** 4:00 is **quarter to** 4.

A **quarter** of an hour **after** 4:00 is **quarter past** 4.

quarter to 4   4:00   quarter past 4

☐ Write the time.

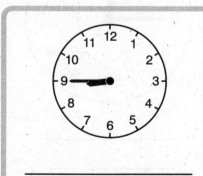

quarter _**past**_ 7

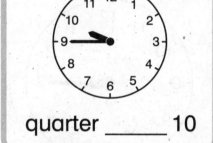

quarter _____ 10

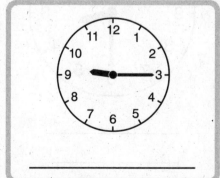

quarter _____ 5

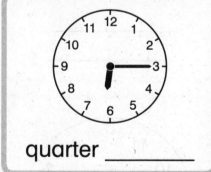

quarter _____

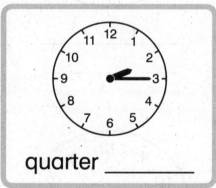

quarter _____

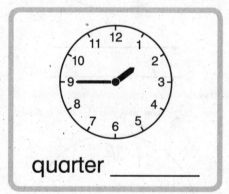

quarter _____

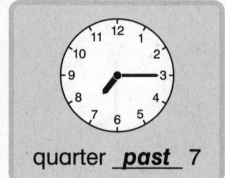

_____

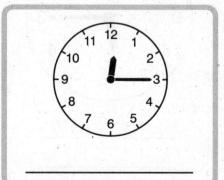

_____

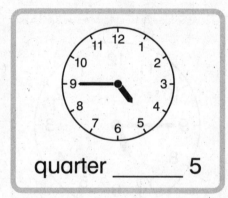

_____

☐ **Write the time in two ways.**

____7____ : ___45___
quarter to 8

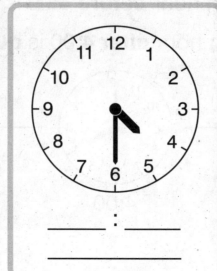

_____ : _____

_____

_____ : _____

_____

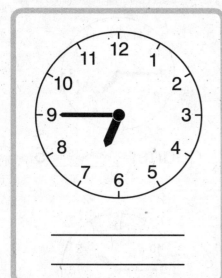

_____

_____

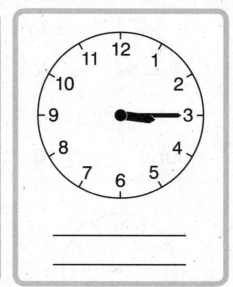

_____

_____

_____

_____

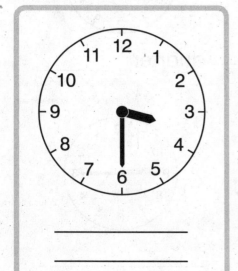

_____

_____

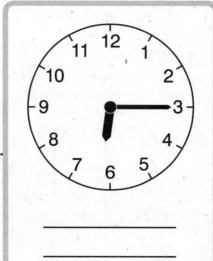

_____

_____

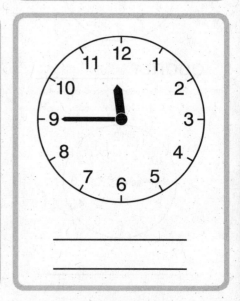

_____

_____

Comparing Areas

☐ Trace the shapes.
☐ Cut them out and compare the areas.
☐ Write **bigger** and **smaller** on each pair.

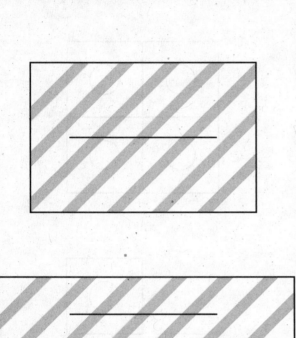

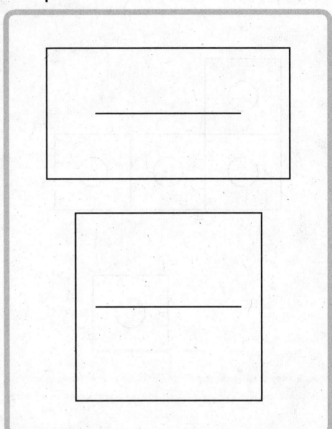

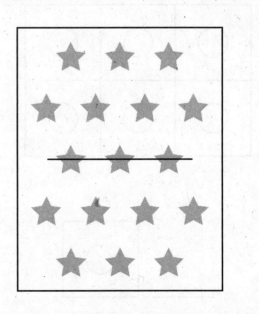

Measuring Area

Use big 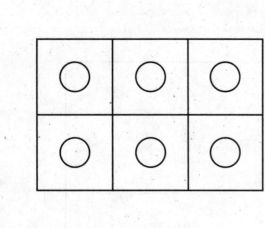 as a unit.

☐ Measure the area.

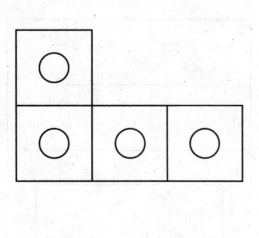

_____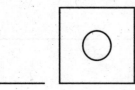

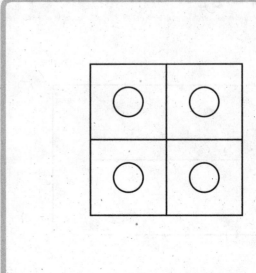

_____

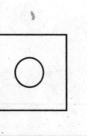

_____

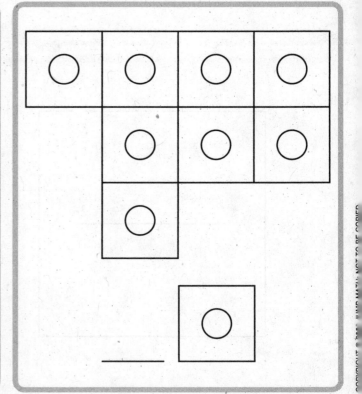

_____

Use big 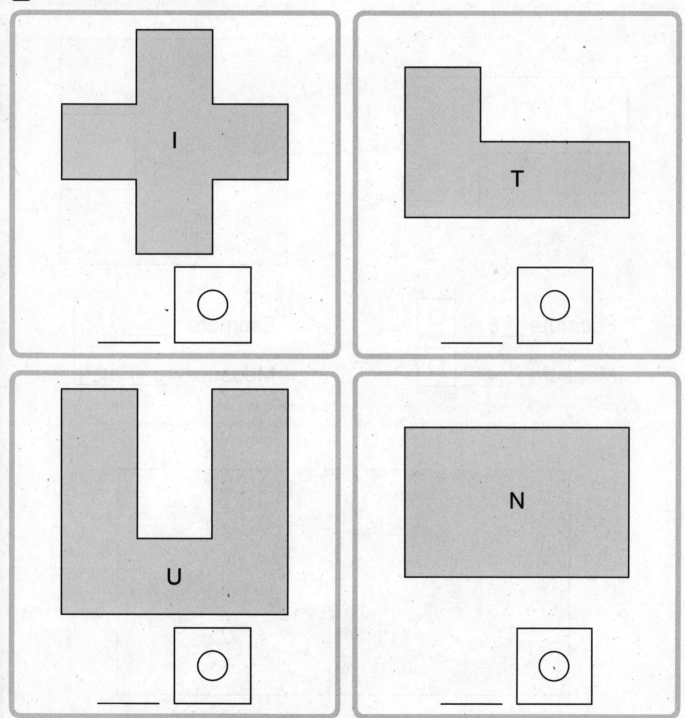 as a unit.

☐ Measure the area.

☐ Order the shapes from biggest to smallest.

_____ _____ _____ _____

Estimate the area.
Check how many big 🎲.

Estimate **5** ○

Measure **4** ○

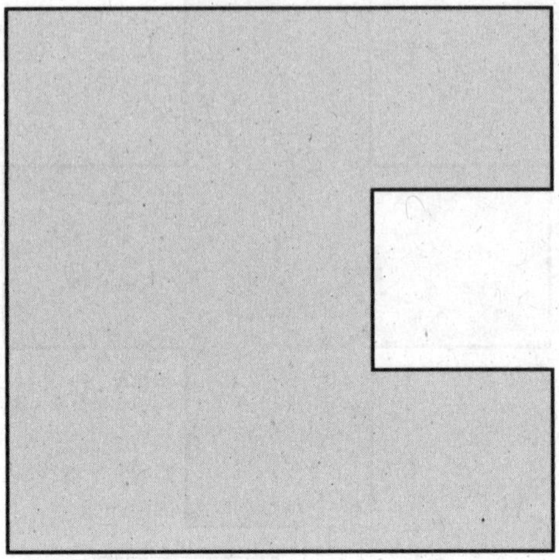

Estimate _____ ○

Measure _____ ○

Estimate _____ ○

Measure _____ ○

Use ▦ as a unit.

☐ Estimate the area.
☐ Measure the area.

	Estimate	Measure
	___ ▦	___ ▦
	___ ▦	___ ▦
	___ ▦	___ ▦
You choose.	___ ▦	___ ▦

Comparing Units of Area

☐ Cover the shape with ⬜ and with ⬜.
How many?

_____ ⬜   _____ ⬜

_____ ⬜   _____ ⬜

_____ ⬜   _____ ⬜

📓 Did it take more ⬜ or more ⬜ to cover the shapes? Why?

Days and Months

☐ Write the days of the week in order.
☐ Circle the days you go to school.

Friday	1.	*Sunday*
Thursday	2.	
Monday	3.	
Saturday	4.	
Wednesday	5.	
~~Sunday~~	6.	
Tuesday	7.	

☐ Unscramble the days.

ridFya	**F**	**r**	**i**	**d**	**a**	**y**	
noMyad	**M**	___	___	**d**	**a**	**y**	
Sduany	___	___	___	**d**	**a**	**y**	
Tduaeys	___	___	___	___	___	___	___
rsudhaTy	___	___	___	___	___	___	___
Syataurd	___	___	___	___	___	___	___
aWdedsney	___	___	___	___	___	___	___

☐ Write the months of the year in order.
☐ Circle the months you go to school.

May	1.	*January*
July	2.	
December	3.	
~~January~~	4.	
March	5.	
November	6.	
September	7.	
June	8.	
February	9.	
October	10.	
August	11.	
April	12.	

☐ Unscramble the months.

yaM ____ ____ ____

eJun ____ ____ ____ ____

lyJu ____ ____ ____ ____

Bonus: ybrFeuar ____ ____ ____ ____ ____ ____ ____ ____

Calendars

☐ Use this calendar to answer the questions.

March 2010

Sunday	Monday	Tuesday	Wednesday	Thursday	Friday	Saturday
	1	2	3	4	5	6
7	8	9	10	11	12	13
14	15	16	17	18	19	20
21	22	23	24	25	26	27
28	29	30	31			

What **day** is…

March 1st? _____ *Monday*

March 16th? _____

March 25th? _____

What **date** is…

the first Wednesday? _____ *March 3rd*

the third Saturday? _____

the second Monday? _____

☐ Use this calendar to answer the questions.

April 2010						
Sunday	**Monday**	**Tuesday**	**Wednesday**	**Thursday**	**Friday**	**Saturday**
		Today		1	2	3
4	5	6	7	8	9	10
11	12	13	14	15	16	17
18	19	20	21	22	23	24
25	26	27	28	29	30	

Today is __T__ __ __ __ day, Ap __ __ __ 6, __ __ __1__ __0__ .

What **day** was it yesterday? _____

What **date** will it be tomorrow? _____

Sayaka has a play date on April 15th.

How many **days** until her play date? _____

Ben's birthday is in exactly one week.

What **day** is his birthday? _____

What **date** is his birthday? _____

A class trip is in exactly 1 month.

What **date** is the trip? _____

Thermometers

We use a **thermometer** to tell how **hot** or **cold** something is.

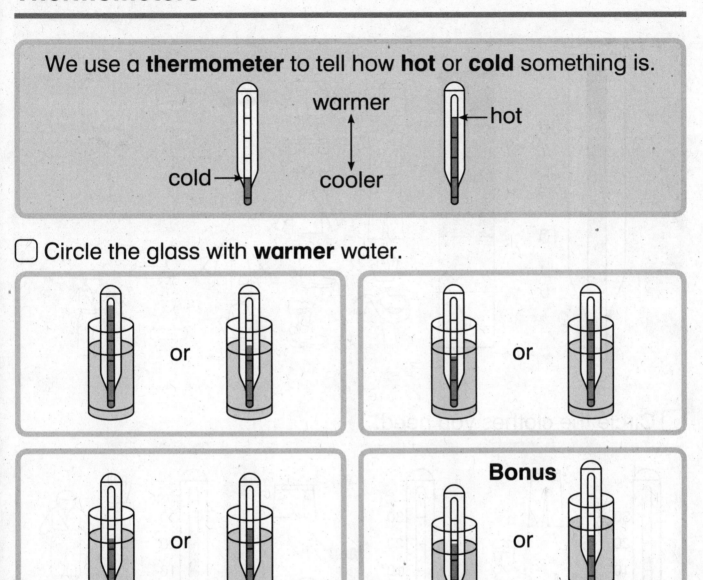

cold

warmer

cooler

hot

☐ Circle the glass with **warmer** water.

or

or

or

Bonus

or

As we heat water, it gets warmer.

☐ What happens 1st, 2nd, and 3rd?

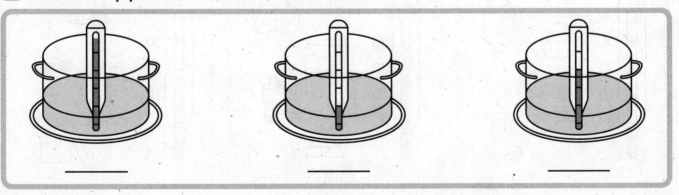

_____   _____   _____

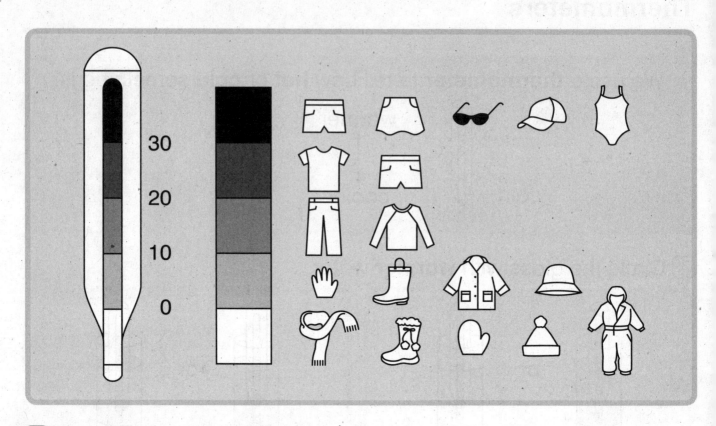

☐ Circle the clothes you need.

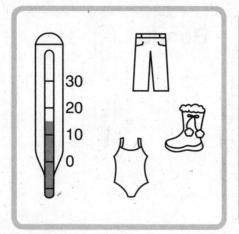

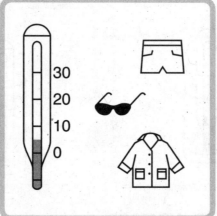

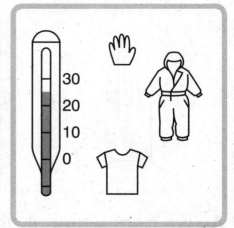

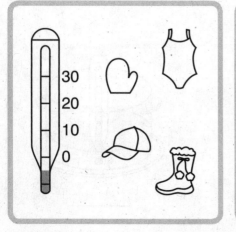

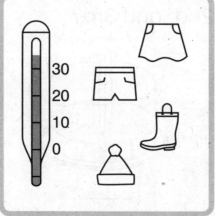

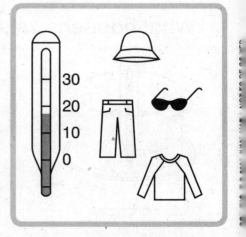

What Holds More?

☐ Write **less than**, **more than**, or **the same as**.

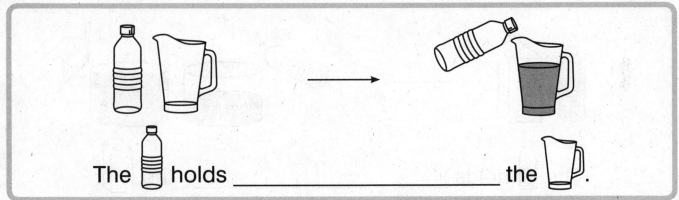

The 🥤 holds _____**less than**_____ the 🥫.

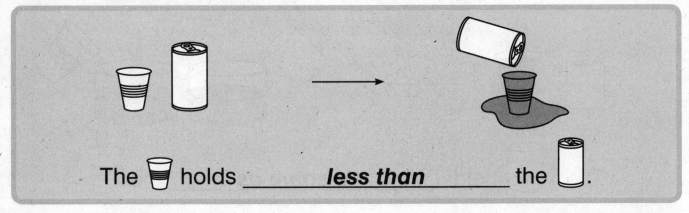

The 🍶 holds _____ the 🫙.

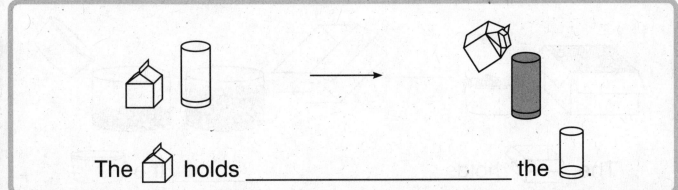

The ⬭ holds _____ the 🫙.

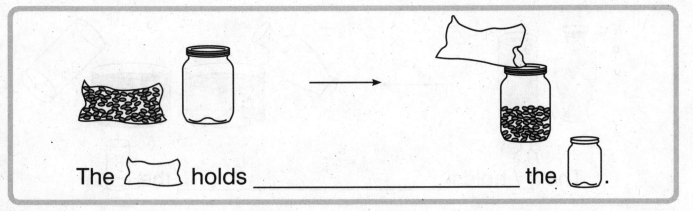

The 🥛 holds _____ the ▯.

Capacity

☐ Write **less than**, **more than**, or **the same as**.

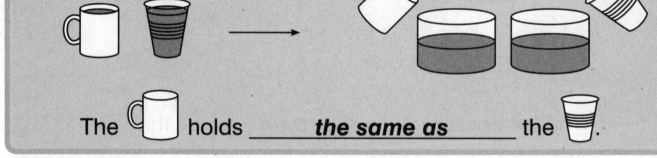

The 🍺 holds _____*the same as*_____ the 🥤.

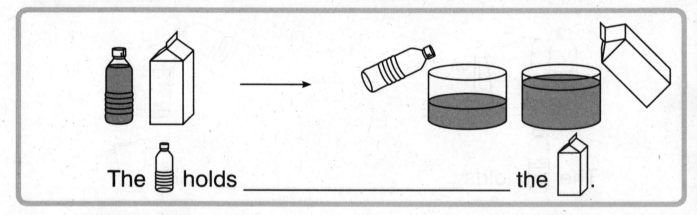

The 🍾 holds _____ the 🥛.

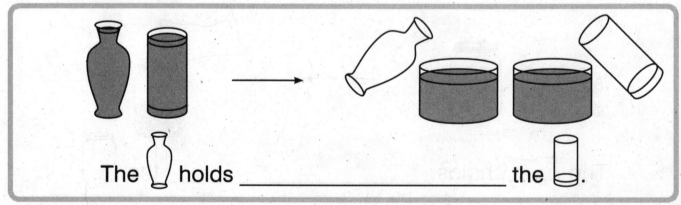

The 🏺 holds _____ the ▯.

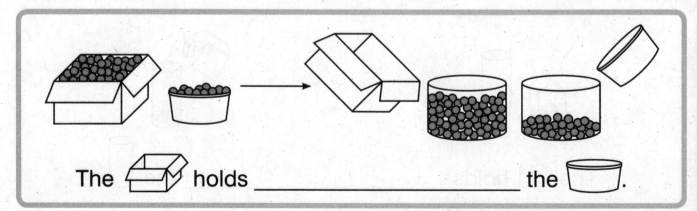

The ▭ holds _____ the ▢.

Measuring Capacity

☐ Circle the container that holds **more**.

☐ Circle the container that holds **less**.

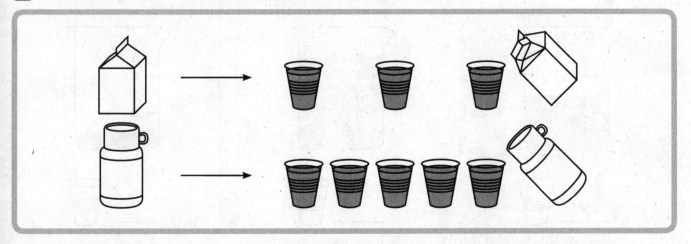

☐ Order the containers from largest (1st) to smallest (3rd).

_____   _____   _____

Measuring Cups

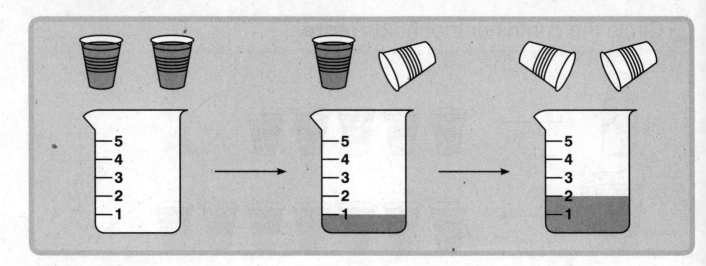

How much water?

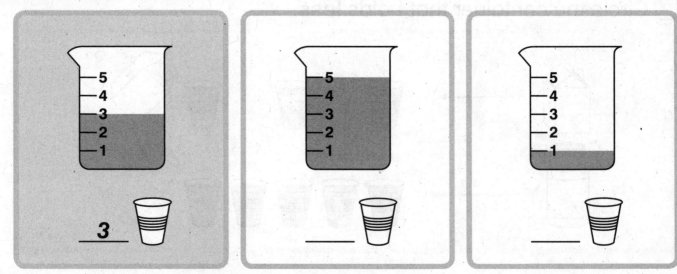

_____3_____

_____

_____

About how much water?

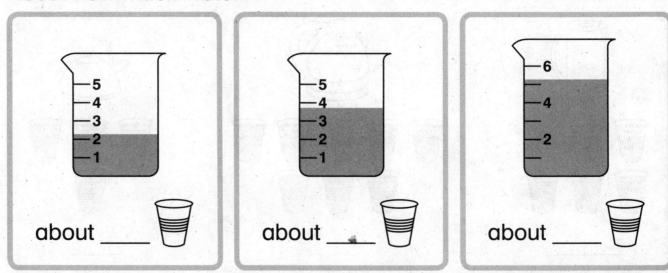

about _____

about _____

about _____

Problems and Puzzles

 turned the clocks around. Can you still tell the time?

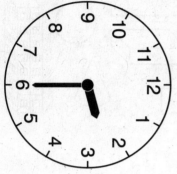   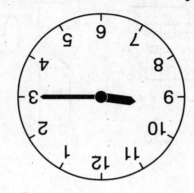   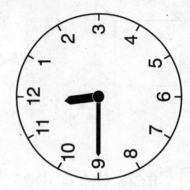

_____   _____   _____

Check your answers by turning the book!

Which clock is wrong? How do you know?

_____

_____

 Is correct? Explain.

 holds 5 .

 holds 3 .

 says: holds more than .

Cubes

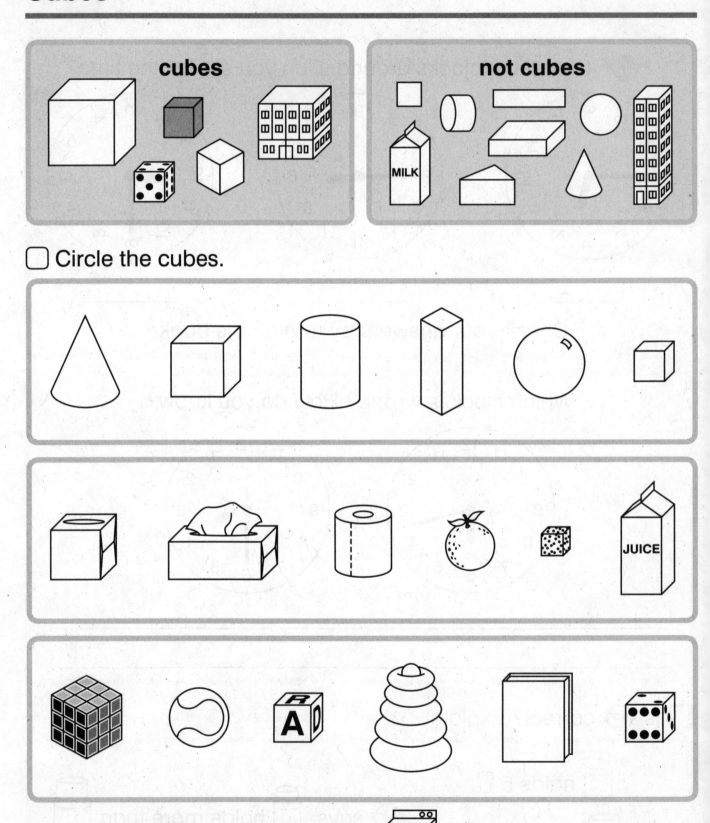

cubes

not cubes

MILK

☐ Circle the cubes.

JUICE

R
A

☐ Find 2 pictures of objects like a 🗔 that are almost cubes.
Glue them into your 📓.

Spheres, Cylinders, and Cones

spheres	not spheres

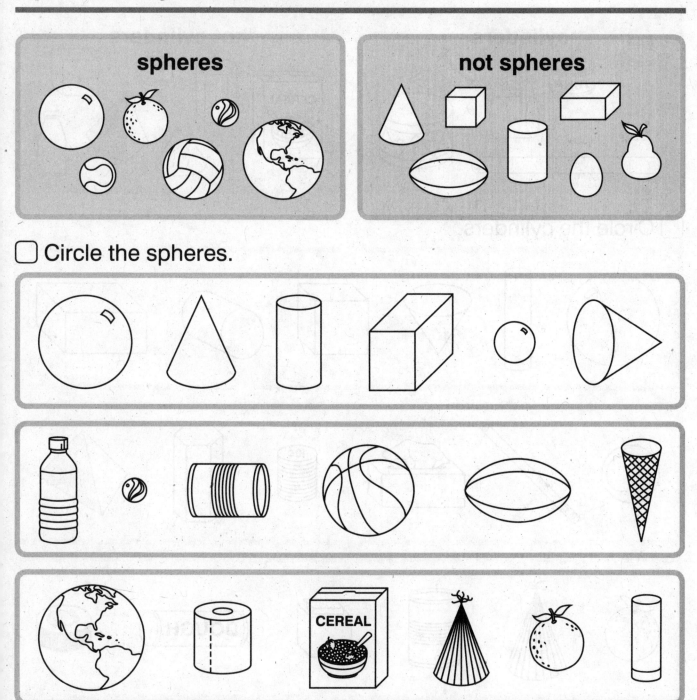

☐ Circle the spheres.

☐ Draw 2 more objects that are almost spheres.

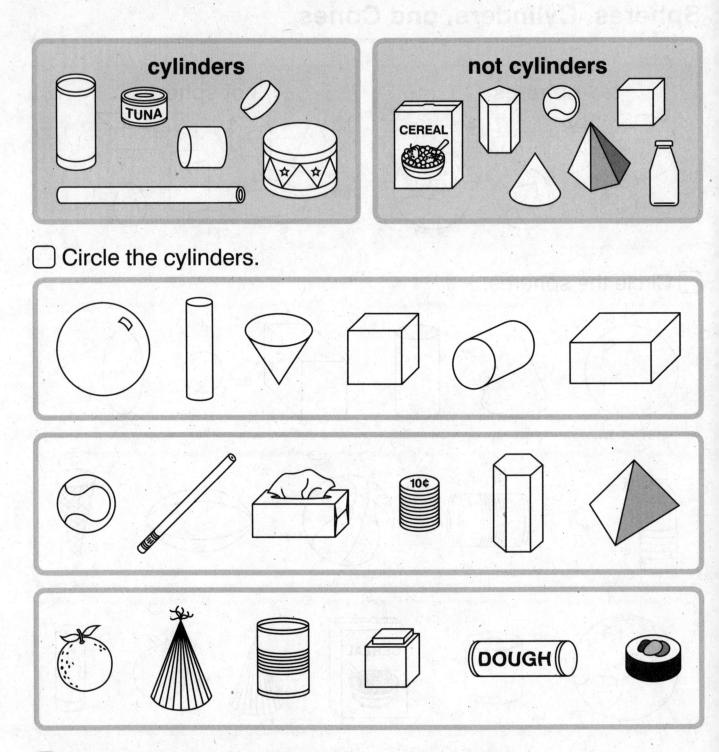

cylinders

TUNA

not cylinders

CEREAL

☐ Circle the cylinders.

10¢

DOUGH

☐ Draw 2 more objects that are almost cylinders.

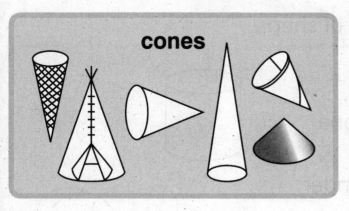

cones

not cones

☐ Circle the cones.

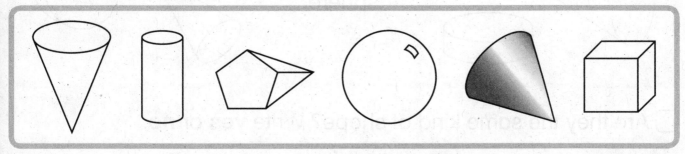

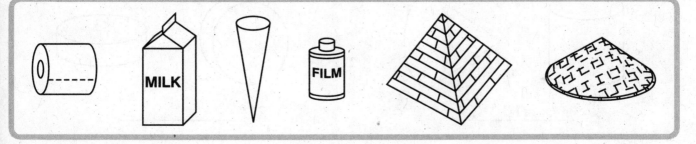

MILK   FILM

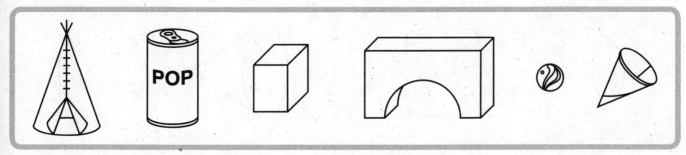

POP

☐ Draw 2 more objects that are almost cones.

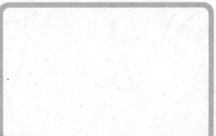

Match the pictures to the kind of shape.

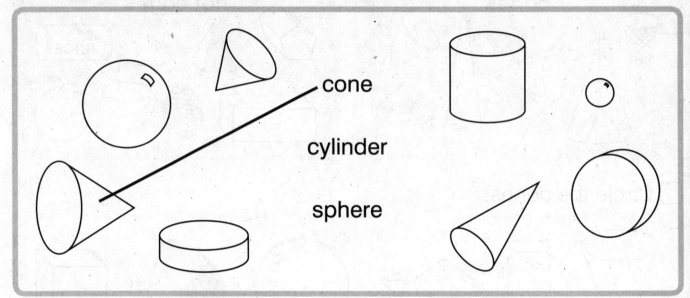

cone

cylinder

sphere

Are they the same kind of shape? Write **yes** or **no**.

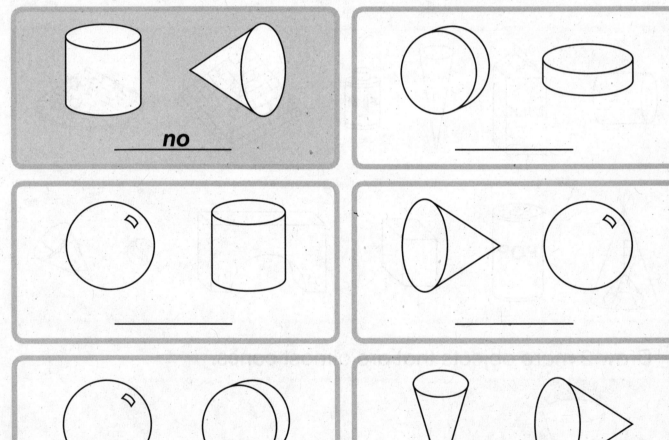

_no_

Pyramids

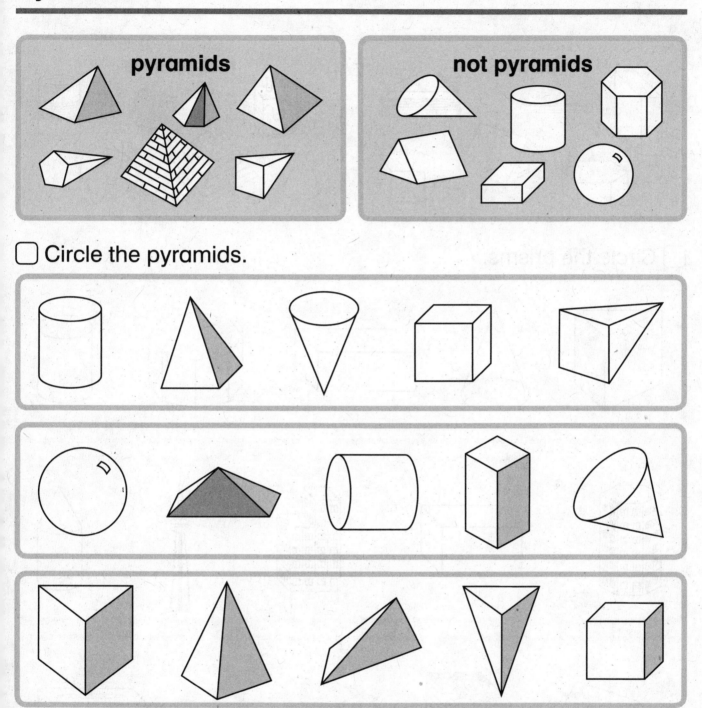

pyramids

not pyramids

☐ Circle the pyramids.

☐ Colour the pyramids in the pictures.

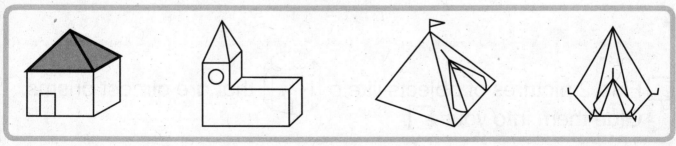

Prisms

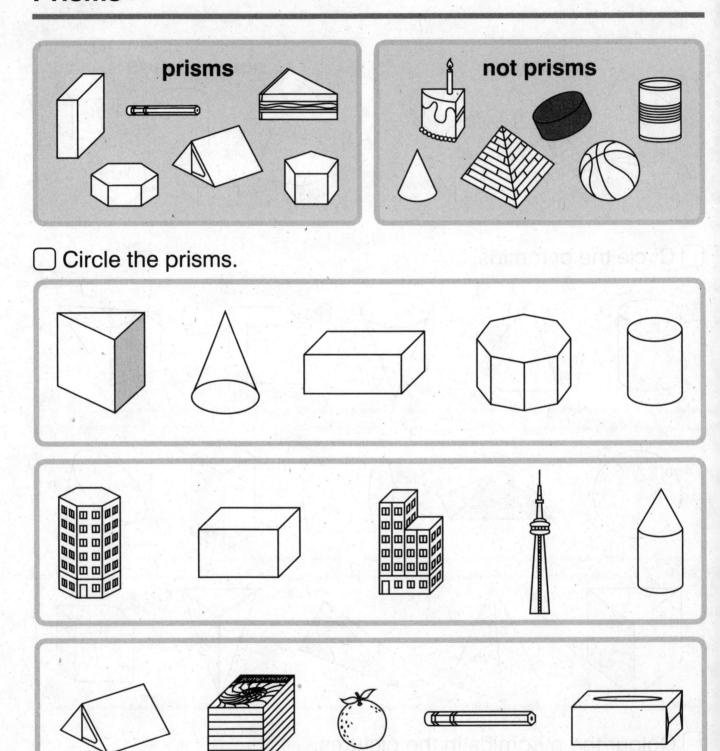

prisms

not prisms

☐ Circle the prisms.

📓 Find 2 pictures of objects like a that are almost prisms. Glue them into your 📓.

Turning 3-D Shapes

Was the object **changed** or **turned**?

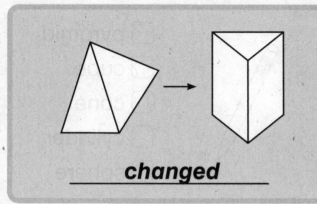
changed

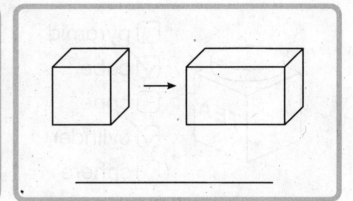
_____

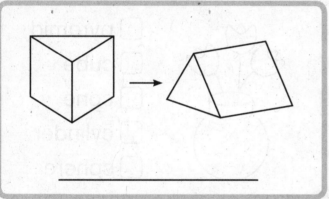
_____

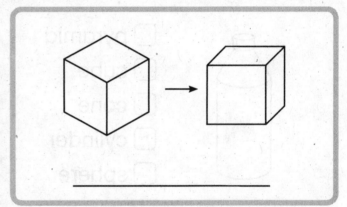
_____

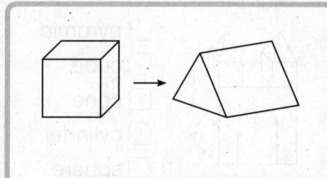
_____

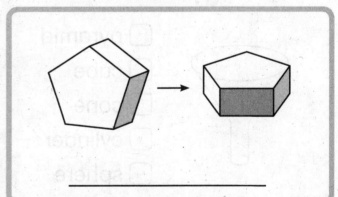
_____

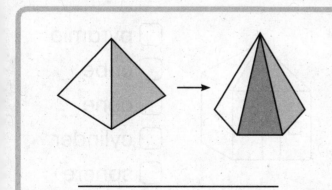
_____

Bonus

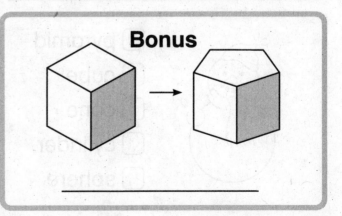
_____

Shapes in Structures

☐ ✓ the shapes you see in the structure.

TEA
- ☐ pyramid
- ☑ cube
- ☐ cone
- ☑ cylinder
- ☐ sphere

- ☐ pyramid
- ☐ cube
- ☐ cone
- ☐ cylinder
- ☐ sphere

- ☐ pyramid
- ☐ cube
- ☐ cone
- ☐ cylinder
- ☐ sphere

- ☐ pyramid
- ☐ cube
- ☐ cone
- ☐ cylinder
- ☐ sphere

- ☐ pyramid
- ☐ cube
- ☐ cone
- ☐ cylinder
- ☐ sphere

- ☐ pyramid
- ☐ cube
- ☐ cone
- ☐ cylinder
- ☐ sphere

- ☐ pyramid
- ☐ cube
- ☐ cone
- ☐ cylinder
- ☐ sphere

- ☐ pyramid
- ☐ cube
- ☐ cone
- ☐ cylinder
- ☐ sphere

☐ Count the figures you see.

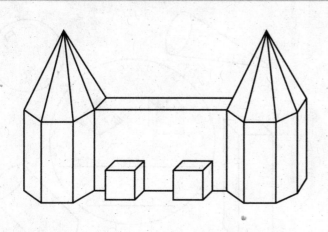

_____ cubes

_____ prisms

_____ pyramids

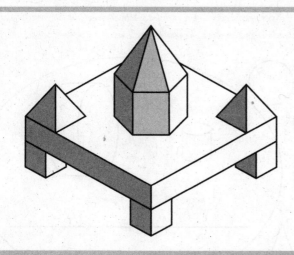

_____ cubes

_____ prisms

_____ pyramids

Bonus

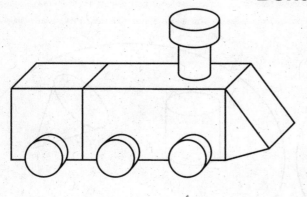

_____ cubes

_____ prisms

_____ pyramids

_____ cylinders

☐ Build your own structure from blocks.
How many of each type did you use?

How are these sorted?

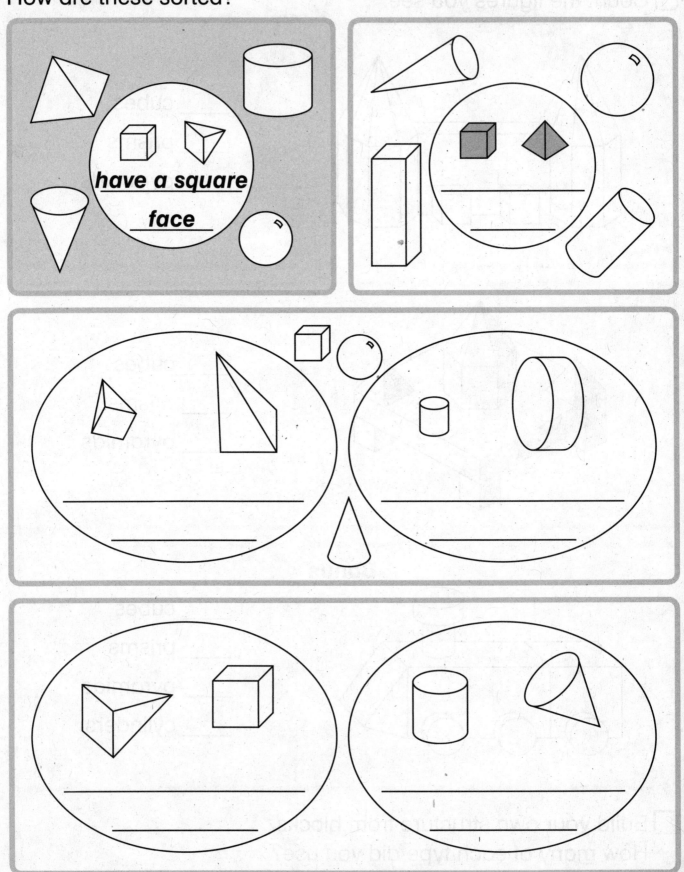

have a square face

Faces

☐ What is the shape of the dark face? Circle it.

☐ **What is the shape of the dark face?** ✗ **it.**

Use real 3-D shapes.

☐ Circle the shapes that have a face that is...

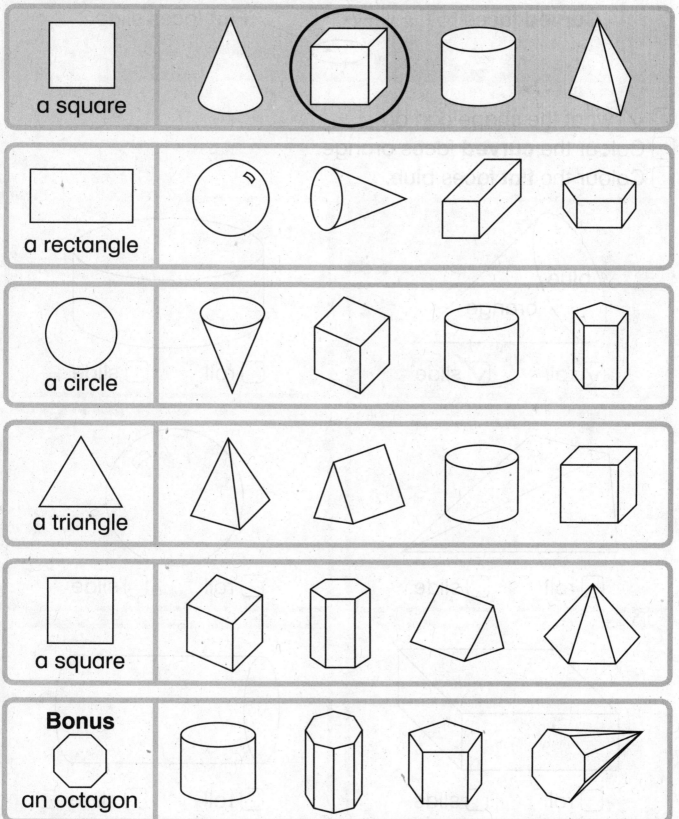

a square

a rectangle

a circle

a triangle

a square

Bonus

an octagon

Roll, Slide, Stack

Curved faces roll. ⟶ **Flat** faces slide.

☐ ✓ what the shape can do.
☐ Colour the **curved** faces orange.
☐ Colour the **flat** faces blue.

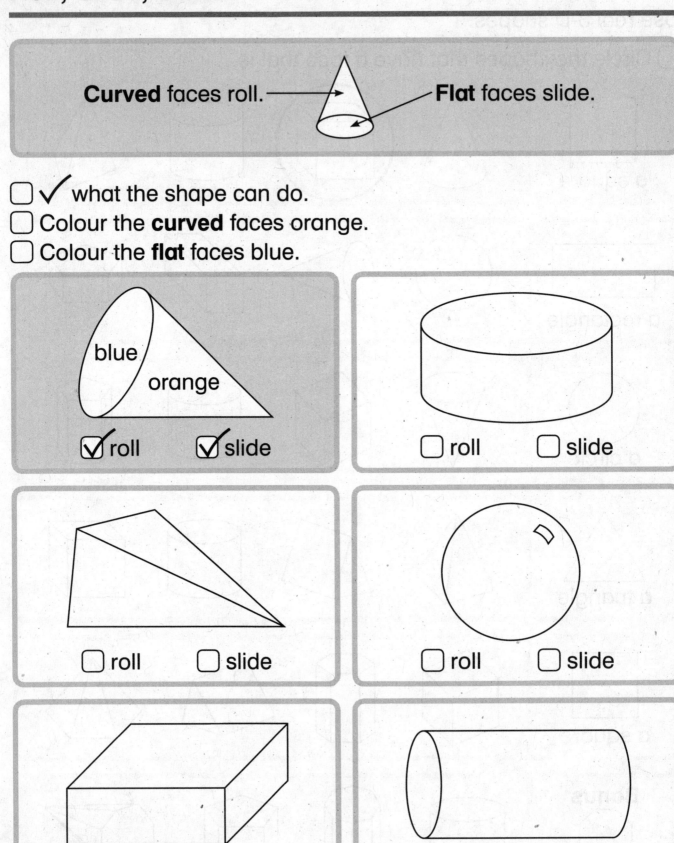

blue
orange
☑ roll   ☑ slide

☐ roll   ☐ slide

☐ roll   ☐ slide

☐ roll   ☐ slide

☐ roll   ☐ slide

☐ roll   ☐ slide

☐ Use the letters to sort the shapes.

| A | B | C | D | E | F |

have a curved face	have only flat faces
A	B

have a ☐ face	have a ○ face

only roll	roll and slide	only slide

large	small

📓 Choose another geometric attribute and sort the shapes again.

Vertices

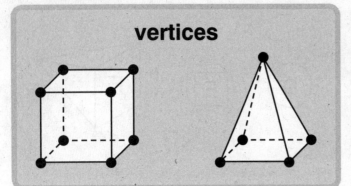

vertices

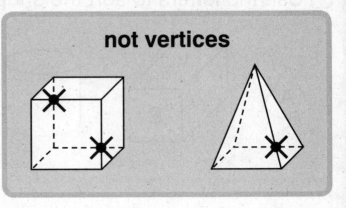

not vertices

☐ Draw a ● on each vertex.
☐ Count the vertices.

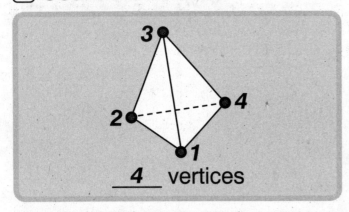

3

2 *4*

1

___4___ vertices

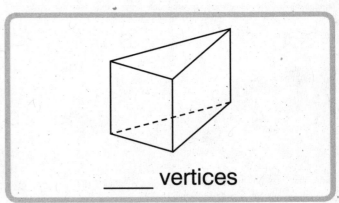

_____ vertices

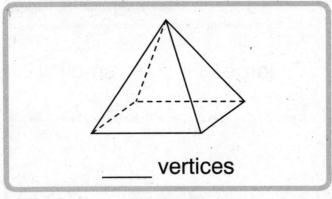

_____ vertices

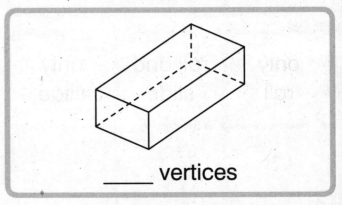

_____ vertices

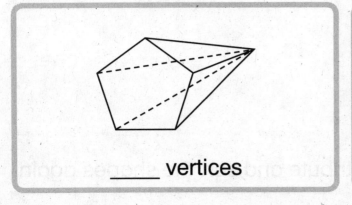

_____ vertices

Bonus

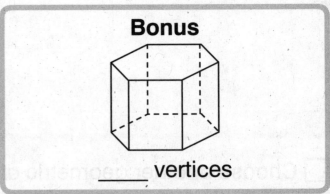

_____ vertices

Edges

This shape has 6 **edges**.

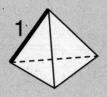 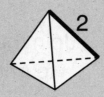 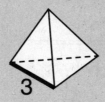   

☐ Count the edges.

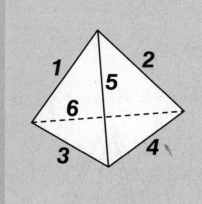

___6___ edges

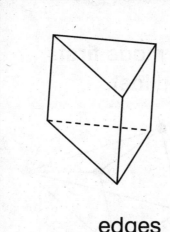

_____ edges

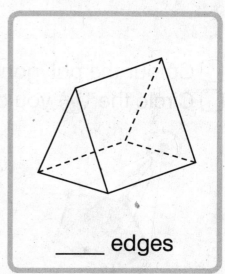

_____ edges

_____ edges

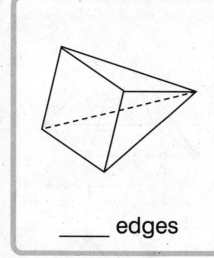

_____ edges

Bonus

_____ edges

Take a real 3-D object.
How many faces meet at each edge?
Compare your answer with a partner.

☐ Make skeletons of pyramids from straws and clay ☽. Follow these steps.

1. Make a polygon.	2. Put a ▭ in each ☽.	3. Join the ▭ to another ☽.
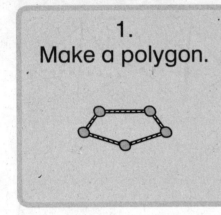	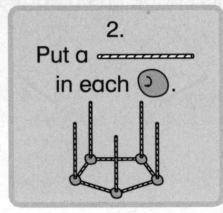	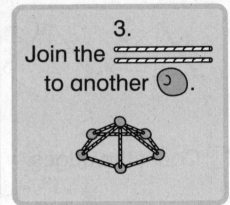

☐ Colour the polygon you made **first**.
☐ Circle the ☽ you added **last**.

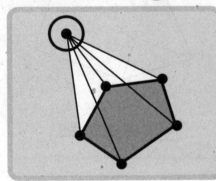
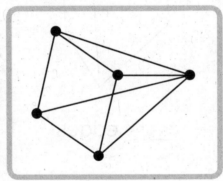
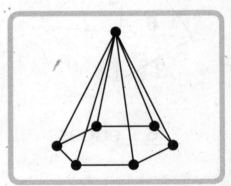

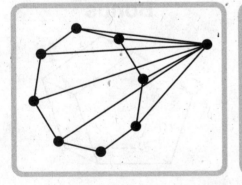
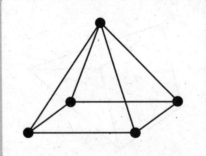
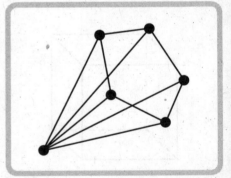

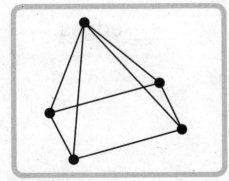
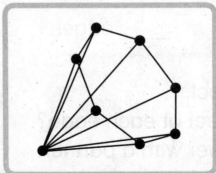
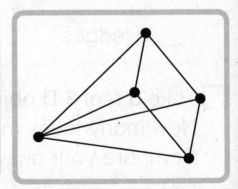

Left, Right, Above, Below

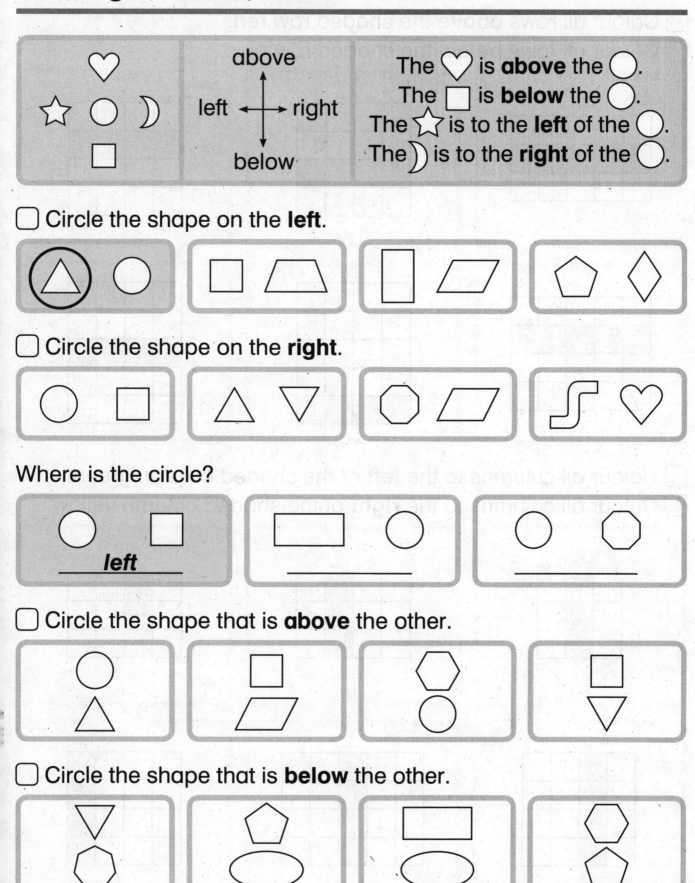

□ Circle the shape on the **left**.

□ Circle the shape on the **right**.

Where is the circle?

left

□ Circle the shape that is **above** the other.

□ Circle the shape that is **below** the other.

☐ Colour all rows **above** the shaded row red.
☐ Colour all rows **below** the shaded row blue.

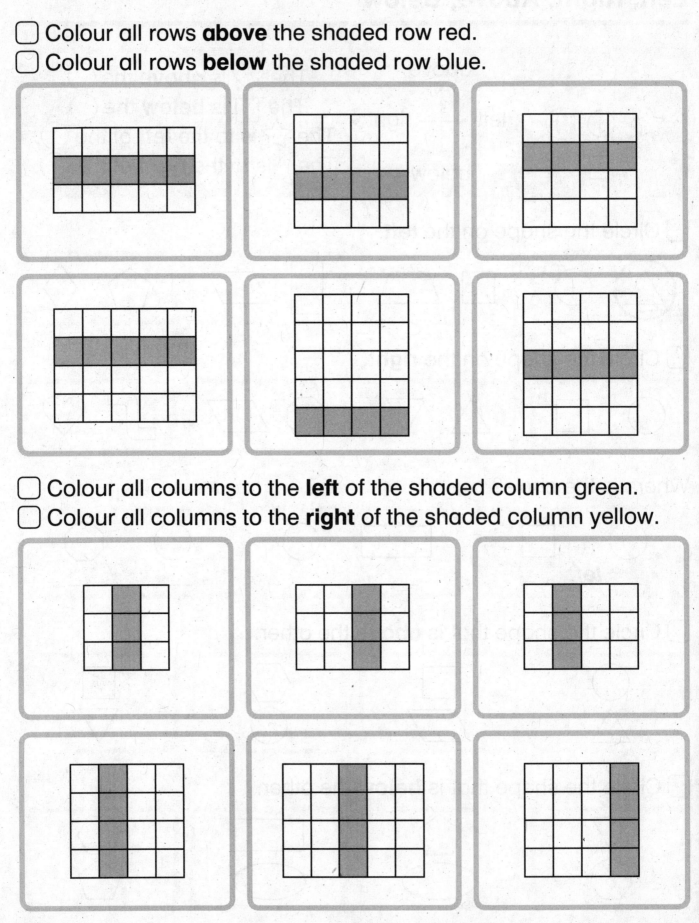

☐ Colour all columns to the **left** of the shaded column green.
☐ Colour all columns to the **right** of the shaded column yellow.

☐ Colour the first 5 squares above the ladybug green.
☐ Colour the first 5 squares below the butterfly green.
☐ Draw a dot in the square to the right of the rocket.
  Colour the square below the dot yellow.
☐ Draw a dot in the square to the left of the balloon.
  Colour the first 3 squares above the dot yellow.
☐ Find the square between the two green columns that is
  directly in the middle and colour it green.
☐ What word do you see? _____

Maps

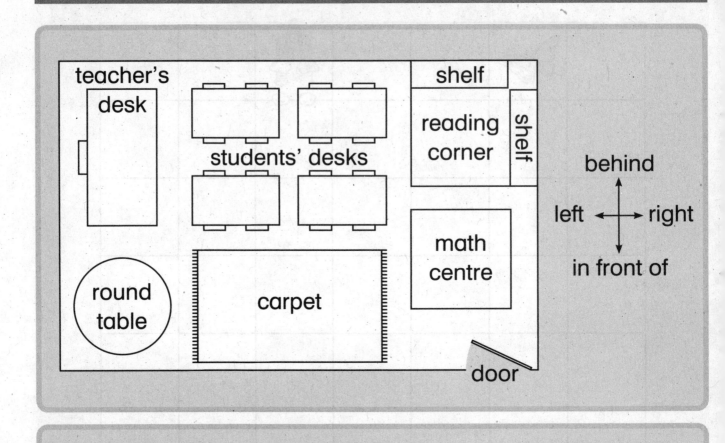

in front of	~~left of~~	right of	behind

☐ Answer the questions.

Where is the teacher's desk? To the _____**left of**_____ the students' desks.

Where is the reading corner? _____ the math centre.

Where is the math centre? To the _____ the carpet.

Where is the carpet? _____ the students' desks.

▤ Write 2 questions about this map.
Ask a friend to answer them.

▤ Draw a map of your classroom. Show where you sit. Write 4 sentences telling where some objects in your classroom are.

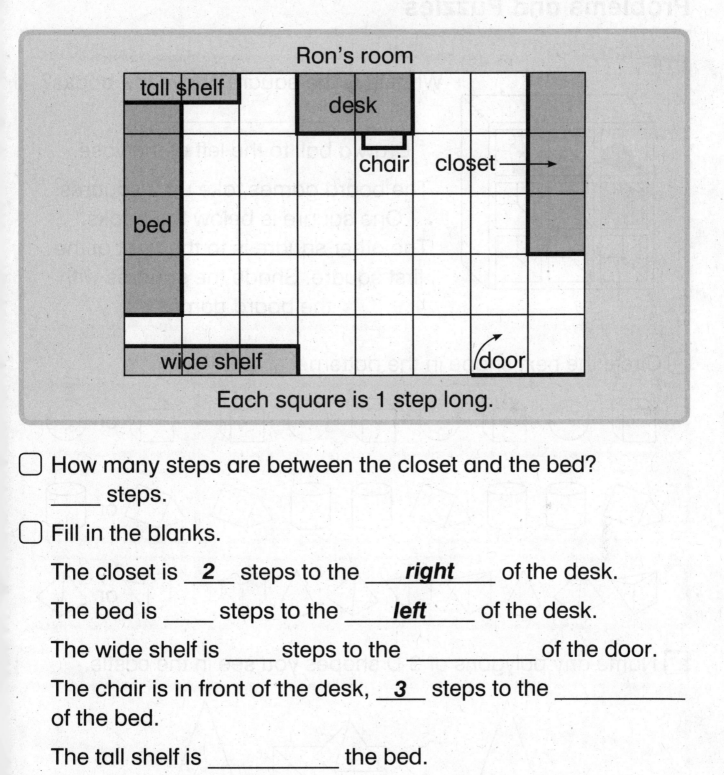

Ron's room

tall shelf

desk

chair   closet ———→

bed

wide shelf   door

Each square is 1 step long.

☐ How many steps are between the closet and the bed?
   ____ steps.

☐ Fill in the blanks.

The closet is __2__ steps to the ____right____ of the desk.

The bed is ____ steps to the ___left___ of the desk.

The wide shelf is ____ steps to the _____ of the door.

The chair is in front of the desk, __3__ steps to the _____
of the bed.

The tall shelf is _____ the bed.

☐ The window is behind the desk. The window is 4 steps long.
   The tall shelf is right beside it. Draw the window.

☐ The beanbag chair is right in front of the window, 1 step
   to the right of the bed. Draw the beanbag chair.

Problems and Puzzles

What is in the square above the books?

_____

Draw a ball to the left of the vase.

The board games take up 2 squares.
One square is below the books.
The other square is to the right of the
first square. Shade the squares with
the board games.

☐ Circle the next shape in the pattern.

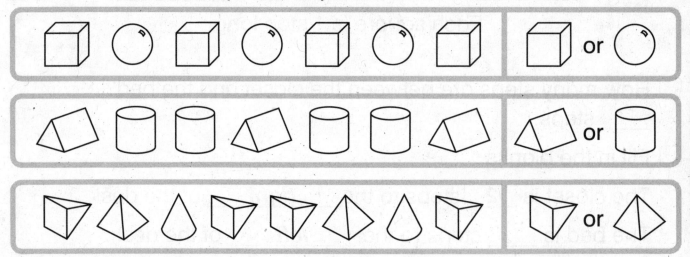

⧚ Name any polygons or 3-D shapes you see in the castle.

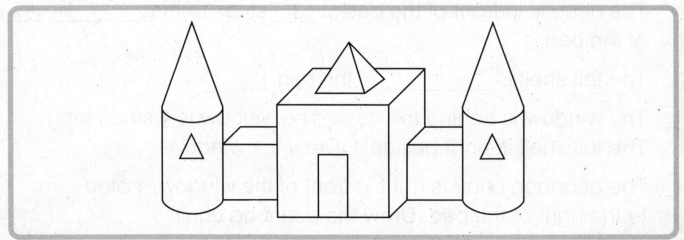

Bar Graphs

How many?

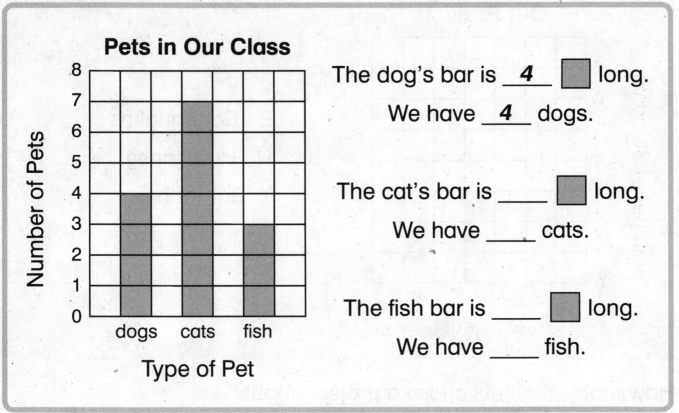

Pets in Our Class

The dog's bar is __4__ 🔲 long.

We have __4__ dogs.

The cat's bar is ____ 🔲 long.

We have ____ cats.

The fish bar is ____ 🔲 long.

We have ____ fish.

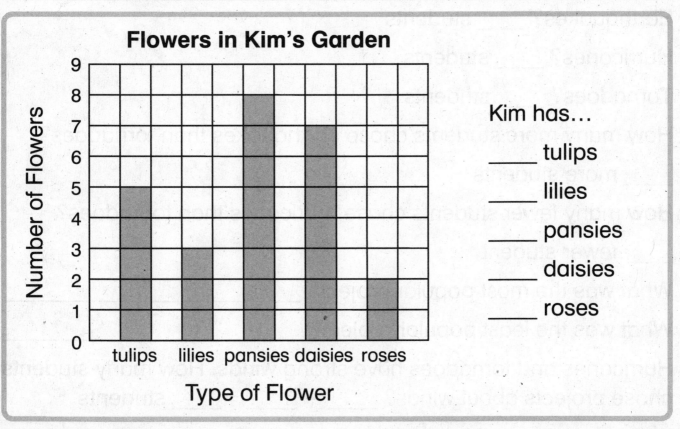

Flowers in Kim's Garden

Kim has…

____ tulips

____ lilies

____ pansies

____ daisies

____ roses

☐ Answer the questions.

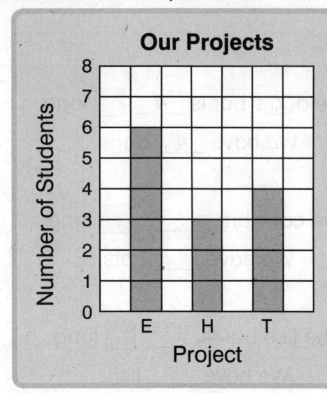

Our Projects

E - Earthquakes

H - Hurricanes

T - Tornadoes

How many students chose a project about…

Earthquakes? _____ students

Hurricanes? _____ students

Tornadoes? _____ students

How many more students chose earthquakes than tornadoes?

_____ more students

How many fewer students chose hurricanes than tornadoes?

_____ fewer student

What was the most popular project? _____

What was the least popular project? _____

Hurricanes and tornadoes have strong winds. How many students chose projects about winds? _____ + _____ = _____ students

☐ Draw a bar graph using the data.
☐ Answer the questions.

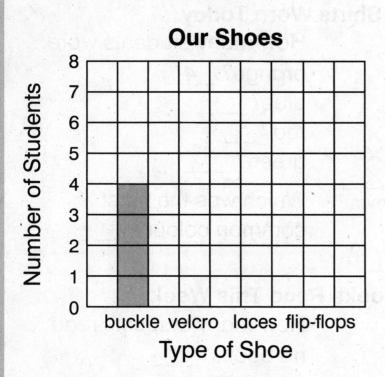

Our Shoes

Number of Students

buckle velcro laces flip-flops
Type of Shoe

buckle	4
velcro	7
laces	8
flip-flops	3

Which bar is tallest?

_____

Which bar is shortest?

_____

Angela's Clothes

Number of Items

_____*skirts*_____ _____ _____
Type of Clothing

Angela has 5 skirts,
7 pants, and
3 pairs of shorts.

How many more
pants than skirts does
Angela have?

_____

Line Plots

☐ Count the **X**s to say how many.

Colour of Shirts Worn Today

Colour of Shirt

orange   blue   red   green

How many students wore…
orange? __4__
blue? ____
red? ____
green? ____

Which was the most common colour? ____

Number of Books Read This Week

Number of Books

0   1   2   3

How many students read…
no books? ____
1 book? ____
2 books? ____
3 books? ____

What is the most common number of books read? ____

Number of Pockets We Have

Number of Pockets

0 1 2 3 4 5 6 7

How many people have…
2 pockets? ____
7 pockets? ____
no pockets? ____

Which number of pockets does nobody have? Circle.

0 1 2 3 4 5 6 7

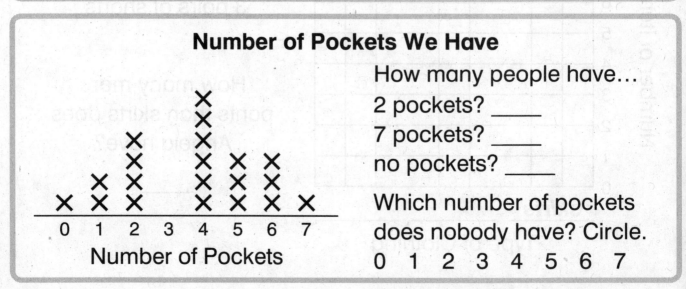

☐ Use the line plots.

Number of Letters in Our Names

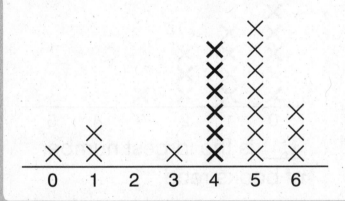

5 people have 3 letters in their names.
Circle the ✗s that show this.

The thick ✗s show that
__6__ people have
__5__ letters in their names.

Number of Buttons on Our Clothes Today

2 people have 1 button on their clothes today.
Circle the ✗s that show this.

The thick ✗s show that
____ people have
____ buttons on their clothes.

Number of People in Our Families

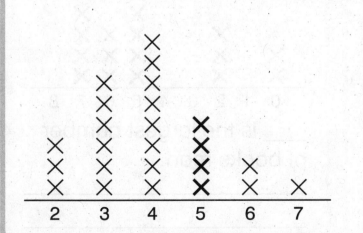

6 people have 3 people in their families.
Circle the ✗s that show this.

The thick ✗s show that

_____

_____

_____

These line plots show the number of books read.

What is the largest number of books read?
How many people read that many books?

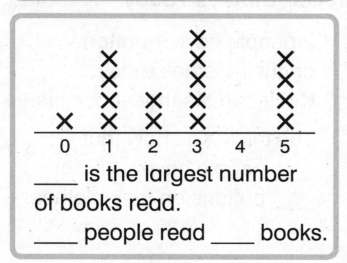

__4__ is the largest number
of books read.
__2__ people read __4__ books.

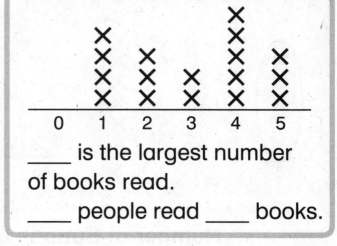

____ is the largest number
of books read.
____ people read ____ books.

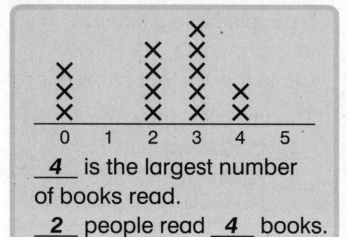

____ is the largest number
of books read.
____ people read ____ books.

____ is the largest number
of books read.
____ person read ____ books.

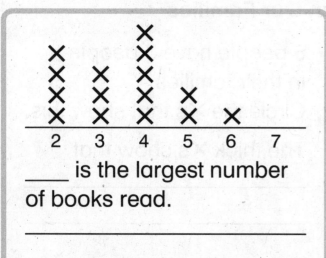

____ is the largest number
of books read.

_____

_____

____ is the largest number
of books read.

_____

_____

Number of Letters in Names

		X	X						
		X	X						
	X	X	X						
	X	X	X						
	X	X	X	X					
	X	X	X	X					
	3	4	5	6					

☐ Count the number of letters in each name below.
☐ Add a blue X to the chart for **Finn**.
☐ Add a red X for **Rowan**.
☐ Add a green X for **Jan**.
☐ Add a column and an orange X for **Jo**.
☐ Add a column and a black X for **Michael**.
☐ Add a brown X for your name.

☐ Answer the questions.

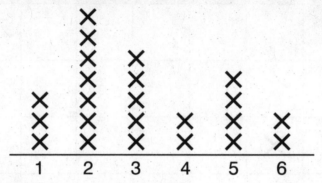

Number of Books We Read This Week

How many people read 4 books? ____ people

How many people read 3 books? ____ people

How many **more** people read 3 books than 4 books?
____ more people

How many **fewer** people read 6 books than 2 books?
____ fewer people read __6__ books than __2__ books.

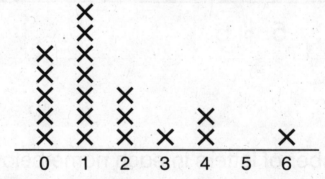

Number of Siblings (Brothers or Sisters)

What is **the largest number** of siblings a person has?
____ siblings

How many people have that many siblings? ____ person

What is **the most common** number of siblings? ____ sibling

How many people have that many siblings? ____ people

Tallies

☐ Write the number or draw the tally.

│	**1**	**││**	**2**	**卌**	**5**	**卌 │**	**6**

│││			4	卌 ││			8

卌 卌		卌 ││││			11

卌 卌 │││			15

卌 卌 卌 ││││			17

	20	卌 卌 卌 卌 ││

	25	卌 卌 卌 卌 卌 卌

☐ Tally the number of objects.
☐ Cross out the objects as you count.

Asking Questions About Data

☐ Ask a question using the words given.

Favourite Classes

gym	🙂	🙂	🙂	🙂	🙂
art	😀	😀			
music	😮	😮	😮		
drama	😎	😎			

how many

How many students

chose gym class?

_____

the same number

Which two classes were

chosen by the same

number of students?

two most popular

What are the two most

popular classes?

_____

Favourite Ice Cream

chocolate	卌 卌
vanilla	‖‖
strawberry	卌 ‖‖

how many

_____

_____

_____

the most popular

_____

_____

_____

the least popular

_____

_____

_____

☐ Ask a question using the words given.
☐ Have a friend answer your question.

Our Hair Colour

Number of Students

5
4
3
2
1

blond   brown   red   black

Hair Colour

---

fewer… than

Question: _**How many fewer students have red hair**_

**than blond hair?**

Answer: _____

_____

---

more… than

Question: _____

_____

Answer: _____

_____

---

the most common

Question: _____

_____

Answer: _____

_____

Surveys

Lina asked her class:

What is your favourite season?

Spring   Summer   Winter

Are there enough choices? yes / no

☐ Explain. _____

_____

What choice should she add? _____

☐ Explain. _____

_____

Miki asked his class:

How many siblings (brothers or sisters) do you have?

0   1   2   3

Dennis has 4 siblings.

Ahmed has 7 siblings.

They could not answer the survey.

☐ Add **one more** choice so that both Ahmed and Dennis
can answer the survey. _____

☐ Ask students in your class: How did you get to school today?
☐ Tally your results.

Title: _____

school bus	
car	
walk	
bike	
scooter	
other	

☐ Make a pictograph. Use ☺.

Title: _____

What did you learn from your survey?

☐ How did most students get to school today?

_____

☐ How many students came that way? ____

☐ Why do you think that way was the most common way of getting to school?

_____

_____

_____

☐ What else does your pictograph show?

_____

_____

_____

☐ Write 2 questions about your data and have a friend answer them.

Question: _____

_____

Answer: _____

_____

Question: _____

_____

Answer: _____

Certain or Impossible?

Certain events **always** happen. 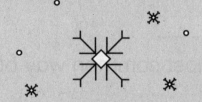 It will get cold in winter.	**Impossible** events **never** happen.  An alien will study in my class.

☐ Sort the events.

I will spin black on this spinner.

I will be older next year.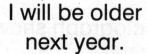

I will be 3 years old next year.

Certain   **Impossible**

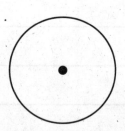
I will spin white on this spinner.

Cookies will grow on trees.

I will roll 1, 2, 3, 4, 5, or 6 on a die.

Likely or Unlikely?

Likely events happen **often**, but not always.

I will go to school in the morning.

Unlikely events can happen, but **not so often**.

I will roll a 3 five times in a row.

☐ Write **likely** or **unlikely**.

I will eat lunch.

likely

A student will be lighter than a teacher.

_____

I will roll a 6 two times in a row.

_____

I will spin black on this spinner.

_____

It will snow in June.

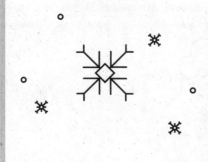

_____

I will take a white cube from this bag.

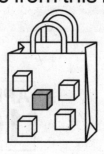

_____

More Likely or Less Likely?

impossible   unlikely   likely   certain

Circle the event that is **more** likely.

A mermaid will teach math.   or   Our teacher will teach math.

A bird will fly.   or   A cow will fly.

I will be hot.   or   I will be hot.

APRIL 10 It will rain in April.   or   APRIL 10 It will snow in April.

More Likely, Equally Likely, or Less Likely?

☐ Compare the events.

| more likely | equally likely | less likely |

Dan will ride a pony.   Dan will ride a T-rex.

__It is more likely that Dan will ride a pony than a T-rex.__

A fish will sing.   Rosa will sing.

It is _____ likely that a fish will sing than _____.

A coin will land on heads.   A coin will land on tails.

It is _____.

I will pull out a grey cube.   I will pull out a white cube.

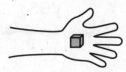 

_____

Problems and Puzzles

Pam asked her friends what pizza topping they like most.

Favourite Pizza Toppings

pepperoni	
mushrooms	
onions	
other	

She found that...

5 friends prefer mushrooms

3 more friends prefer pepperoni than mushrooms

5 more friends prefer onions than pepperoni

4 friends chose other

☐ Finish the pictograph to show Pam's data.

☐ Pam orders pizza for a party. Which 2 toppings should she choose? _____ and _____

Is the spinner equally likely to land on dots and stripes?

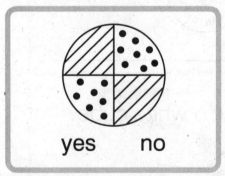

yes   no

yes   no

yes   no

☐ Explain one of your answers. _____

_____

Probability and Data Management 2-16